Henry Percy

Our cashier's scrap-book

Being bank notes, new and old, for general circulation

Henry Percy

Our cashier's scrap-book
Being bank notes, new and old, for general circulation

ISBN/EAN: 9783337108960

Printed in Europe, USA, Canada, Australia, Japan

Cover: Foto ©Suzi / pixelio.de

More available books at **www.hansebooks.com**

OUR

CASHIER'S SCRAP-BOOK;

BEING

BANK NOTES,

NEW AND OLD,

FOR GENERAL CIRCULATION.

A PORTFOLIO OF BANK ANECDOTES AND INCIDENTS,

QUEER, CURIOUS, ODD, LUDICROUS, TOUCHING.

POETRY BY AND ABOUT BANKERS; "CAPITAL" ITEMS; CONVERSA-
TIONS WITH CUSTOMERS, AND FACTS AND STATISTICS OF GENERAL
INTEREST ABOUT BANKS, ACCUMULATED FROM ALL THE
WORLD, DURING A PERSONAL EXPERIENCE OF TEN
YEARS BEHIND A BANK COUNTER.

COMPILED BY

H. C. PERCY,

Cashier of the Home Savings Bank, Norfolk, Va.

WITH ILLUSTRATIONS AND PORTRAITS.

NEW YORK:

Copyright, 1879, by

G. W. Carleton & Co., Publishers,

LONDON: S. LOW, SON & CO.

MDCCCLXXIX.

Dedication.

TO THE ARMY OF BANK CASHIERS,

THEIR CLERKS, MESSENGERS AND ASSISTANTS,

AND

TO THE DEAR PUBLIC WHO HANDLE OUR MONEY,

AND WHO KEEP, OR OUGHT TO KEEP,

BANK ACCOUNTS,

IN THE HOPE THAT THEY MAY PROVE ENTERTAINING AND INSTRUCTIVE,

THESE "BANK NOTES"

ARE RESPECTFULLY INSCRIBED, BY

THE COMPILER.

"Thare iz advice enuff now laying around loose to run three just such worlds as this; what we are suffering most for is sum more good examples."

—Josh Billings.

"A single farthing is the semina of wealth—the seed of a golden progeny."   —Anon.

"The contents of his book seemed to be as heterogeneous as those of the witches' caldron in Macbeth. It was here a finger and there a thumb, toe of frog and blind-worm's sting, with his own gossip poured in like 'baboons' blood,' to make the medley 'slab and good.'"

—Irving.

CONTENTS.

—

Contents.

PREFATORY.

SAID a student to his preceptor, "Doctor, let us write a book." "A capital idea," replied the doctor; "we'll put in all that I know, and all that you don't know, and we'll make quite a book!"

In a similar humor this work was conceived. It represents, so far as the compiler is concerned, the net result of a thousand half-hours, snatched from a busy life, and used by way of recreation to fasten the good things he has read, heard, suffered, or found out during his ten years of bank life, from his customers, his correspondents and the fraternity at large. Claiming only to be a SCRAP-BOOK, the sharp-penned critics are notified to pass by on the other side. All the glory hereunto appertaining is due the distinguished men from whose works we quote, the banks whose success is noted, the host of able cashiers who have so cleverly taken the stand and recited their stories, and to the good books from which so many items have been coolly embezzled. The compiler desires only to be recognized as the humble string which ties all this together.

The idea is by no means a new one. It is older than Rome; for did not the great Cæsar compile a similar book in which he set down the *bon-mots* of Cicero? And Quintillian tells of a three-volume work by his freedman, entitled, "De Jocis Ciceronis." Then, too, we have the "Anecdota Greca," from the old Greek Fathers, and a

"Thesaurus Novus Anecdotorum," by Martene and Durand, besides the "Anecdota" of Becker, Bachmann and Heinbach. The ancients having established and enjoyed so excellent a precedent, no apology is needed in A. D. 1879, for bringing forth this "Banker's Tickler," or "Bankiana," which may partially illustrate the thought of D'Israeli, "Every class of readers requires a book adapted to itself."

It is impossible that a volume of so modest dimensions should contain all that is worth preserving in this line. The world couldn't contain the books that might be made up from the daily history of queer, eccentric, sad, curious, ludicrous, astonishing illustrations of poor, weak human nature, with which the country's bankers are conversant. But here is, at least, enough for one sitting, and quite sufficient to show the scope of the banker's profession (?) as well as the charmed sort of life he leads.

Such readers as experience pain because of the omission of incidents they expected to find herein, are respectfully invited to forward the same in time for publication in Volume II. of this work, which has already been contemplated by

H. C. P.

Norfolk, Va., *October* 1, 1879.

THANK YOU!

I hereby make hearty acknowledgment to the editors and publishers of the following works for kind permission to "extract" many good things from their works:

Appleton's Cyclopedia of Business Anecdotes.
Harper's Drawer.
Spofford's American Year Book.
Rhodes' Journal of Banking.
Bankers' Magazine.
The Safeguard.

H. C. P.

THE

BANKERS' SCRAP-BOOK.

———————•———————

POET BANKERS.

"Poeta nascitur, non fit."

In Dickens' immortal Christmas Carol is charmingly
set forth this pen-painting of one who approaches the
world's average ideal of a banker, the last man on earth
to be guilty of doing homage at the Muses' shrine :

"Oh! But he was a tight-fisted hand at the grind-
stone, Scrooge! a squeezing, wrenching, grasping,
scraping, clutching, covetous old sinner! Hard and
sharp as flint, from which no steel had ever struck out
generous fire ; secret, and self-contained, and solitary as
an oyster. The cold within him froze his old features,
nipped his pointed nose, shriveled his cheek, stiffened
his gait ; made his eyes red, his thin lips blue ; and
spoke out shrewdly in his grating voice. A frosty rime
was on his head, and on his eyebrows, and his wiry
chin. He carried his own low temperature always
about with him ; he iced his office in the dog-days ; and
didn't thaw it one degree at Christmas. No warmth
could warm, no wintry weather chill him. No wind
that blew was bitterer than he, no falling snow was more

[15]

intent upon its purpose, no pelting rain less open to
entreaty.   Foul weather didn't know where to have him.
The heaviest rain, and snow, and hail, and sleet, could
boast of the advantage over him in only one respect.
They often 'came down' handsomely, and Scrooge
never did."

It is presumed the following random selections and
contributions of poetry from bankers more or less distinguished, will come as a gentle surprise to many
readers, who will not only enjoy them, but haply may
thus be brought to a better mind, and led to conclude
that, after all, the "bulls" and the "bears" are far less
savage than they are painted.

With the leisure hours for study possessed by many
of the profession, and their constant attrition with every
variety and idiosyncracy of character in the business
world, why should not bankers, as a *class*, be able to
exhibit fair intellectual culture, and perchance add
somewhat to the world's treasury of mental wealth?   Be
it the Scrap-Book's mission to show that they have done
so.

SAMUEL ROGERS,

ENGLAND'S BANKER POET.

The name of SAMUEL ROGERS is worthy of place in
the front rank of bankers who have been favored with
the sweet gift of song.   He was for some time a banker
of London, but retired from the business after a brief
experience, and devoted himself to literature.   For a
half-century, his house (No. 22) in St. James's Place was

a famous resort of literary men, and a repository of many art-treasures. He died in 1855, at the advanced age of 92 years. His "Pleasures of Memory," "Voyage of Columbus," and "Table-Talk" have given him a world-wide reputation, and the charming poems on "Italy" are outward evidences of an inner soul-life immeasurably above bank-notes and bullion. We quote from his published works the following choice poems and fragments :

THE SCHOOL-HOUSE.

The school's lone porch, with reverend mosses gray,
Just tells the pensive pilgrim where it lay.
Mute is the bell that rung at peep of dawn,
Quickening my truant feet across the lawn :
Unheard the shout that rent the noontide air,
When the slow dial gave a pause to care.
Up springs, at every step, to claim a tear,
Some little friendship formed and cherished here !
And not the lightest leaf, but trembling teems
With golden visions and romantic dreams !

MELANCHOLY.

Go ! you may call it madness, folly—
    You shall not chase my gloom away ;
There's such a charm in melancholy,
    I would not if I could be gay.

Oh, if you knew the pensive pleasure
    That fills my bosom when I sigh,
You would not rob me of a treasure
    Monarchs are too poor to buy !

ON A. TEAR.

Oh ! that the chemist's magic art
   Could crystallize this sacred treasure !
Long should it glitter near my heart,
   A secret source of pensive pleasure.

The little brilliant, ere it fell,
   Its luster caught from Chloe's eye ;
Then, trembling, left its coral cell—
   The spring of Sensibility.

Sweet drop of pure and pearly light !
   In thee the rays of Virtue shine ;
More calmly clear, more mildly bright,
   Than any gem that gilds the mine.

Benign restorer of the soul !
   Who ever fly'st to bring relief,
When first we feel the rude control
   Of Love or Pity, Joy or Grief.

The sage's and the poet's theme,
   In every clime, in every age ;
Thou charm'st, in Fancy's idle dream,
   In Reason's philosophic page.

That very law that molds a tear,
   And bids it trickle from its source—
That law preserves the earth a sphere,
   And guides the planets in their course.

A WISH.

Mine be a cot beside the hill ;
A beehive's hum shall soothe my ear ;
A willowy brook that turns a mill,
With many a fall, shall linger near.

The swallow, oft, beneath my thatch,
Shall twitter from her clay-built nest;
Oft shall the pilgrim lift the latch,
And share my meal, a welcome guest.

Around my ivied porch shall spring
Each fragrant flower that drinks the dew :
And Lucy at her wheel shall sing
In russet gown and apron blue.

The village church, among the trees,
Where first our marriage vows were given,
With merry peals shall swell the breeze,
And point with taper spire to heaven.

VENICE.

There is a glorious City in the Sea !
The sea is in the broad, the narrow streets,
Ebbing and flowing, and the salt sea-weed
Clings to the marble of her palaces.
No track of men, no footsteps to and fro,
Lead to her gates.   The path lies o'er the sea,
Invisible ; and from the land we went,
As to a floating city—steering in,
And gliding up her streets as in a dream,
So smoothly, silently—by many a dome,
Mosque-like, and many a stately portico,
The statues ranged along an azure sky ;
By many a pile, in more than eastern splendor,
Of old the residence of merchant-kings ;
The fronts of some, though time had shattered them,
Still glowing with the richest hues of art,
As though the wealth within them had run o'er.

TO THE BUTTERFLY.

Child of the sun ! pursue thy rapturous flight,
Mingling with her thou lov'st in fields of light ;
And, where the flowers of Paradise unfold,
Quaff fragrant nectar from their cups of gold.
There shall thy wings, rich as an evening sky,
Expand and shut with silent ecstacy !
Yet wert thou once a worm, a thing that crept
On the bare earth, then wrought a tomb and slept.
And such is man ! soon from his cell of clay
To burst a seraph in the blaze of day.

———

PLEASURE, that comes unlooked for, is thrice welcome ;
And if it stir the heart, if aught be there
That may hereafter, in a thoughtful hour
Wake but a sigh, 'tis treasured up among
The things most precious ; and the day it came
Is noted as a white day in our lives.

———•———

CHARLES SPRAGUE.

This American poet was born in Boston, 1791. He
was pre-eminently a self-made man, having had no
school advantages after his thirteenth year. After a few
years' experience as clerk and partner in dry-goods and
grocery stores, in 1819 he accepted the position of
Teller in the State Bank of Boston. In 1824 he was
elected to the cashiership of the Globe Bank, which
important position he filled for forty years, with an

integrity and old-fashioned honesty which do his memory as great honor as do the graceful productions of his pen. His poem on "Curiosity," delivered in 1829 before the Phi Beta Kappa society in Cambridge, is considered his best production.

A complete revised collection of his poems was published in 1876 by A. Williams & Co., Boston, through whose kind permission we copy a few specimens of his work.

In 1826, on July 4th, he pronounced a stirring ode at the centennial celebration of Boston, beginning :

> FIFTY years have rolled away,
> Since that high, heroic day,
> When our fathers, in the fray,
>   Struck the conquering blow !
> Praise to them—the bold who spoke ;—
> Praise to them—the brave who broke
> Stern oppression's galling yoke,
>   FIFTY YEARS AGO !

One of Mr. Sprague's sweetest poems is the following, written after the death of his infant son, Charles James, on the anniversary of his birth :

CHARLES JAMES.

> There is a spot—'tis holy ground
>   To those who weep,
> Where, hushed beneath each lonely mound,
>   Death's moldering victims sleep.

Friend, sister, brother, there are laid,
    From sorrows free ;
And there a clay-cold bed is made
    For thee, Sweet Boy ! for thee.

Those little hands thou'lt raise no more
    To meet my arms ;
Thou'rt gone ! the bitter wind passed o'er,
    And withered all thy charms.

Forever gone life's active spark,
    The blood's warm thrill ;
Thy bright blue eyes are closed and dark,
    Thy merry laugh is still.

I've sat me by thy cradle's side,
    And joyed to trace,
Blind fool ! with all a father's pride,
    Thy future earthly race.

Fancy beheld thee good and wise,
    Honor's proud theme,
Truth's sturdy prop, Fame's noble prize,
    But, oh ! 'twas all a dream.

There came an hour—with me 'twill live
    Till life depart ;
Time's vaunted skill no balm can give,
    Remembrance wrings my heart.

'Twas when I watched, with curdling blood,
    Each stifled breath ;
'Twas when on that pale forehead stood
    The boding damp of death.

'Twas when the tyrant's grasp, so cold,
    Chilled life's young tide ;

'Twas when those eyes that last glance rolled—
    'Twas when my poor boy died.

The sigh will rise, in manhood's spite,
    The tears will roll ;
Grief round me draws her mental night,
    And desolates my soul.

Yet let my stricken heart be taught
    That thou'rt in peace ;
That lesson, with true wisdom fraught,
    Should bid each anguish cease.

If there's a refuge-place at last,
    For man t' enjoy, .
There may I meet, earth's trials past,
    My Charles, my cherub boy !

CURIOSITY.

[FRAGMENTS.—THE ENTIRE POEM COVERS THIRTY-TWO PAGES.]

It came from Heaven—it reigned in Eden's shades—
It roves on earth—and every walk invades :
Childhood and age alike its influence own,
It haunts the beggar's nook, the monarch's throne ;
Hangs o'er the cradle, leans above the bier,
Gazed on old Babel's tower—and lingers here.

To all that's lofty, all that's low it turns,
With terror curdles and with rapture burns ;
Now feels a seraph's throb, now, less than man's,
A reptile tortures, and a planet scans ;
Now idly joins in life's poor, passing jars,
Now shakes creation off, and soars beyond the stars.

    *   *   *   *   *

Behold the sick man in his easy-chair ;
Barred from the busy crowd and bracing air,
How every passing trifle proves its power
To while away the long, dull, lazy hour !
As down the pane the rival rain-drops chase,
Curious he'll watch to see which wins the race ;
And let two dogs beneath his window fight,
He'll shut his Bible to enjoy the sight.

*   *   *   *   *

Nor even to life, nor death, nor time confined—
The dread hereafter fills the exploring mind ;
We burst the grave, profane the coffin's lid,
Unwisely ask of all so wisely hid ;
Eternity's dark record we would read—
Mysteries unraveled yet by mortal creed ;
Of life to come, unending joy and woe,
And all that holy wranglers dream below ;
To find their jarring dogmas out we long,
Or which is right, or whether all be wrong ;
Things of an hour, we would invade His throne,
And find out Him, the Everlasting One !

*   *   *   *   *

O Thou, whose fingers raised us from the dust,
Till there we sleep again, be this our trust :
This sacred hunger marks the immortal mind,
By Thee 'twas given, for Thee, for Heaven, designed ;
There the rapt spirit, from earth's grossness freed,
Shall see, and know, and be like Thee indeed.

———

" How cold he hearkens to some bankrupt's woe,
  Nods his wise head, and cries—' I told you so !' "

THE WINGED WORSHIPPERS.

d to two swallows that flew into Chauncey Place Church
during divine service.]

Gay, guiltless pair,
What seek ye from the fields of Heaven ?
Ye have no need of prayer,
Ye have no sins to be forgiven.

Why perch ye here,
Where mortals to their Maker bend?
Can your pure spirits fear
The God ye never could offend ?

Ye never knew
The crimes for which we come to weep.
Penance is not for you,
Blessed wanderers of the *upper deep*.

To you 'tis given
To wake sweet Nature's untaught lays :
Beneath the arch of Heaven,
To chirp away a life of praise.

Then spread each wing,
Far, far above, o'er lakes and lands,
And join the choirs that sing
In yon blue dome not reared with hands.

Or, if ye stay,
To note the consecrated hour,
Teach me the airy way,
And let me try your envied power.

Above the crowd,
On upward wings could I but fly,
2

I'd bathe in yon bright cloud,
And seek the stars that gem the sky.

'Twere Heaven indeed,
Through fields of trackless light to soar,
On Nature's charms to feed,
And Nature's own great God adore.

————

TO MY CIGAR.

Yes, social friend, I love thee well,
In learned doctor's spite ;
Thy clouds all other clouds dispel,
And lap me in delight.

By thee, they cry, with phizzes long,
My years are sooner passed ;
Well, take my answer, right or wrong,
They're sweeter while they last.

And oft, mild friend, to me thou art
A monitor, though still ;
Thou speak'st a lesson to my heart,
Beyond the preacher's skill.

Thou'rt like the man of worth, who gives
To goodness every day,
The odor of whose virtue lives,
When he has passed away.

When, in the lonely evening hour,
Attended but by thee ;
O'er history's varied page I pore,
Man's fate in thine I see.

Oft as thy snowy column grows,
    Then breaks and falls away,
I trace how mighty realms thus rose,
    Thus tumbled to decay.

Awhile, like thee, the hero burns,
    And smokes and fumes around,
And then, like thee, to ashes turns,
    And mingles with the ground.

Life's but a leaf, adroitly rolled,
    And Time's the wasting breath,
That, late or early, we behold,
    Gives all to dusty death.

From beggar's frieze to monarch's robe,
    One common doom is passed :
Sweet Nature's works, the swelling globe,
    Must all burn out at last.

And what is he who smokes thee now ?—
    A little moving heap,
That soon, like thee, to fate must bow,
    With thee in dust must sleep.

But though thy ashes downward go,
    Thy essence rolls on high ;
Thus, when my body must lie low,
    My soul shall cleave the sky.

Mr. Sprague retired from his long cashiership in 1864, to the quiet enjoyment of his home, where, amid friends and domestic pleasures, his remaining years were passed until January 22, 1875, when, after a short and painless illness, he quietly passed away, in the eighty-fourth year of his age.

Among the papers of the late Rev. John Pierpont was found a half-sheet neatly filed and indorsed, and addressed in the handwriting of (the late) Charles Sprague, then cashier, inclosing a promissory note for fifteen hundred dollars, dated " Boston, 25 Augt., 1832," signed by Jno. Pierpont, and indorsed by a Boston publisher prominent at that time.   On the face of the note is written, " Paid, Feb. 28, 1833."   Within, also in Mr. Sprague's handwriting, is the following couplet :

" Behold a wonder seldom seen by men,
 Lines *of no value* from John Pierpont's pen."

The churl, who holds it heresy to *think*,
Who loves no music but the dollar's clink,
Who laughs to scorn the wisdom of the schools,
And deems the first of poets first of fools,
Who never found what good from science grew,
Save the grand truth, that one and one make two,—
'Tis he, across whose brain scarce dares to creep
Aught but thrift's parent pair—to get, to keep.

WILLIAM ROSCOE,

THE POET BANKER.

After Mr. Roscoe had retired to private life, he was earnestly solicited to enter a banking-house, the officers of which desired the attention of a person possessed of a great business capacity and talent. He had already acted as the confidential adviser of the house when in difficulty, and had rendered it valuable assistance. Yielding to the earnest request of his friends he became a partner in said house, and for a time devoted himself exclusively to its concerns. Some seven years after, owing to the demands of the time, and the scarcity of specie, the house was forced to suspend. At his solicitation, the creditors of the firm allowed them six years in which to discharge their debts. During all this period Mr. Roscoe's labors were unremitted. To meet their obligations, however, the private property of the members of the firm had to be sold, and under the most unfavorable circumstances. It was during this season of trial that Mr. Roscoe wrote the following celebrated and immortal sonnet, so well known to all who read the English language, and so evincive of his resignation during trials so severe :

ON PARTING WITH HIS BOOKS.

As one, who, destined from his friends to part,
Regrets his loss, but hopes again ere-while,
To share their converse and enjoy their smile,
And tempers as he may affliction's dart ;
Thus, loved associates ! chiefs of elder art !
Teachers of wisdom ! who could once beguile
My tedious hours, and lighten every toil,
I now resign you—nor with fainting heart ;
For, pass a few short years, or days, or hours,
And happier seasons may their dawn unfold,
And all your sacred fellowship restore ;
When, freed from earth, unlimited its powers,
Mind shall with mind direct communion hold,
And kindred spirits meet to part no more.

EDMUND CLARENCE STEDMAN.

The poems of Mr. Stedman have become household words everywhere. He was a poet, and many of his best efforts appeared, long before he thought of a banker's life; indeed, he did not enter Wall street until thirty years of age. Born in Hartford, Connecticut, in 1833, he removed to New York in 1855, and soon after became a writer for the Tribune. As a journalist, he found no time to write books: so in 1864 he joined the New York Stock Exchange—burning his journalistic ships behind him—and has since been known as a stock-broker and banker, whose evenings and vacations are devoted to literature pure and simple. His books, all of which have appeared since he became a Wall street man, are— "Poems, Lyric and Idyllic;" "Alice of Monmouth and other Poems;" "Complete Poems" (1873); and "Victorian Poems;" critical studies (1875); besides many fugitive pieces which have appeared in the newspapers.

By consent of the accomplished author and his publishers (*Houghton, Osgood & Company, Boston*) we give several specimens of his work.

TOUJOURS AMOUR.

Prithee tell me, Dimple-Chin,
At what age does Love begin?
Your blue eyes have scarcely seen
Summers three, my fairy queen,

But a miracle of sweets,
Soft approaches, sly retreats,
Show the little archer there,
Hidden in your pretty hair ;
When did'st learn a heart to win ?
Prithee tell me, Dimple-Chin !

" Oh !" the rosy lips reply,
" I can't tell you if I try.
'Tis so long I can't remember,
Ask some younger lass than I !"

Tell, O tell me, Grizzled-Face,
Do your heart and head keep pace ?
When does hoary Love expire,
When do frosts put out the fire ?
Can its embers burn below
All that chill December snow ?
Care you still soft hands to press,
Bonny heads to smooth and bless?
When does Love give up the chase?
Tell, O tell me, Grizzled-Face !

" Ah !" the wise old lips reply,
" Youth may pass and strength may die ;
But of Love I can't foretoken :
Ask some older sage than I !"

THE DOORSTEP.

The conference-meeting through at last,
  We boys around the vestry waited
To see the girls come tripping past,
  Like snow-birds willing to be mated.

Not braver he that leaps the wall
    By level musket-flashes litten,
Than I, who stepped before them all
    Who longed to see me get the mitten.

But no, she blushed and took my arm !
    We let the old folks have the highway,
And started toward the Maple Farm
    Along a kind of lovers' by-way.

I can't remember what we said,
    'Twas nothing worth a song or story ;
Yet that rude path by which we sped,
    Seemed all transformed and in a glory.

The snow was crisp beneath our feet,
    The moon was full, the fields were gleaming ;
By hood and tippet sheltered sweet,
    Her face with youth and health was beaming.

The little hand outside her muff—
    O sculptor, if you could but mould it !—
So lightly touched my jacket-cuff,
    To keep it warm I had to hold it

To have her with me there alone,—
    'Twas love and fear and triumph blended.
At last we reached the foot-worn stone
    Where that delicious journey ended.

The old folks, too, were almost home ;
    Her dimpled hand the latches fingered
We heard the voices nearer come,
    Yet on the doorstep still we lingered.

She shook her ringlets from her hood,
  And with a "Thank you, Ned," dissembled ;
But yet I knew she understood
  With what a daring wish I trembled.

A cloud passed kindly overhead,
  The moon was slyly peeping through it,
Yet hid its face, as if it said,
  "Come, now or never ! do it ! *do it !*"

My lips till then had only known
  The kiss of mother and of sister,
But somehow, full upon her own
  Sweet, rosy, darling mouth—I kissed her !

Perhaps 'twas boyish love, yet still,
  O listless woman, weary lover !
To feel once more that fresh, wild thrill
  I'd give—but who can live youth over ?

———

'THE UNDISCOVERED COUNTRY."

    Could we but know
The land that ends our dark, uncertain travel,
  Where lie those happier hills and meadows low,—
Ah, if beyond the spirit's inmost cavil,
  Aught of that country could we surely know,
        Who would not go ?

    Might we but hear
The hovering angels' high imagined chorus,
  Or catch, betimes, with wakeful eyes and clear,
One radiant vista of the realm before us,—
  With one rapt moment given to see and hear,
        Ah, who would fear ?

  2*

Were we quite sure
To find the peerless friend who left us lonely,
Or there, by some celestial stream as pure,
To gaze in eyes that here were love-lit only,—
This weary mortal coil, were we quite sure,
Who would endure?

———

ISRAEL FREYER'S BID FOR GOLD.

FRIDAY, SEPTEMBER 24, 1869.

Zounds! how the price went flashing through
Wall street, William, Broad street, New!
All the specie in all the land
Held in one Ring by a giant hand—
For millions more it was ready to pay,
And throttle the street on hangman's day.
Up from the Gold Pit's nether hell,
While the innocent fountain rose and fell,
Loud and higher the bidding rose,
And the bulls, triumphant, faced their foes.
It seemed as if Satan himself were in it;
Lifting it—one per cent a minute—
Through the bellowing broker, there amid,
Who made the terrible, final bid!
High over all, and ever higher,
Was heard the voice of Israel Freyer,—
A doleful knell in the storm-swept mart,
"Five millions more! and for any part
I'll give One Hundred and Sixty!"

Israel Freyer—the Government Jew—
Good as the best—soaked through and through
With credit gained in the year he sold

Our Treasury's precious hoard of gold ;
Now through his thankless mouth rings out
The leaguers' last and cruellest shout !
Pity the shorts ?   Not they, indeed,
While a single rival's left to bleed !
Down come dealers in silks and hides,
Crowding the Gold Room's rounded sides,
Jostling, trampling each other's feet,
Uttering groans in the outer street ;
Watching, with upturned faces pale,
The scurrying index mark its tale ;
 Hearing the bid of Israel Freyer,—
 That ominous voice, would it never tire ?
" Five millions more !—for any part,
(If it breaks your firm, if it cracks your heart,)
 I'll give One Hundred and Sixty !"

One Hundred and Sixty !   Can't be true !
What will the bears-at-forty do ?.
How will the merchants pay their dues ?
How will the country stand the news ?
What'll the banks—but listen ! hold !
In screwing upward the price of gold
To that dangerous, last, particular peg,
They had killed their Goose with the Golden Egg !
Just there the metal came pouring out,
All ways at once, like a water-spout,
Or a rushing, gushing, yellow flood,
That drenched the bulls wherever they stood !
Small need to open the Washington main,
Their coffer-dams were burst with the strain !
 It came by runners, it came by wire,
 To answer the bid of Israel Freyer,
It poured in millions from every side,

And almost strangled him as he cried,—
  "I'll give One Hundred and Sixty !"

Like Vulcan after Jupiter's kick,
Or the aphoristical Rocket's stick,
Down, down, down, the premium fell,
Faster than this rude rhyme can tell !
Thirty per cent. the index slid,
Yet Freyer still kept making his bid,—
"One Hundred and Sixty for any part !"
—The sudden ruin had crazed *his* heart,
Shattered his senses, cracked his brain,
And left him crying again and again,—
Still making his bid at the market's top
(Like the Dutchman's leg that never could stop,)
"One Hundred and Sixty—Five Millions more !"
Till they dragged him, howling, off the floor.
    The very last words that seller and buyer
    Heard from the mouth of Israel Freyer—
A cry to remember long as they live—
Were, "I'll take Five Millions more ! I'll give—
    I'll give One Hundred and Sixty !"

Suppose (to avoid the appearance of evil)
There's such a thing as a Personal Devil,
It would seem that his Highness here got hold
For once, of a bellowing Bull in Gold !
Whether bull or bear, it wouldn't much matter
Should Israel Freyer keep up his clatter
On earth or under it (as, they say,
He is doomed) till the general Judgment Day,
When the Clerk, as he cites him to answer for't,
Shall bid him keep silence in that Court !
But it matters most, as it seems to me,
That my countrymen, great and strong and free,

So marvel at fellows who seem to win,
That if even a Clown can only begin
By stealing a railroad, and use its purse
For cornering stocks and gold, or—worse—
For buying a Judge and Legislature,
And sinking still lower poor human nature,
The gaping public, whatever befall,
Will swallow him, tandem, harlots, and all !
While our rich men drivel and stand amazed
At the dust and pother his gang have raised,
And make us remember a nursery tale
Of the four-and-twenty who feared one snail.

What's bred in the bone will breed, you know ;
Clowns and their trainers, high and low,
Will cut such capers, long as they dare,
While honest Poverty says its prayer.
But tell me what prayer or fast can save
Some hoary candidate for the grave,
The market's wrinkled Giant Despair,
Muttering, brooding, scheming there,
Founding a college or building a churcn
Lest Heaven should leave him in the lurch !
Better come out in the rival way,
Issue your scrip in open day,
And pour your wealth in the grimy fist
Of some gross-mouthed, gambling pugilist ;
Leave toil and poverty where they lie,
Pass thinkers, workers, artists, by ;
Your pot-house fag from his counters bring
And make him into a Railway King !
Between such Gentiles and such Jews
Little enough one finds to choose :
Either the other will buy and use,

Eat the meat and throw him the bone,
And leave him to stand the brunt alone.

—Let the tempest come, that's gathering near,
And give us a better atmosphere !

———◆———

THE CASHIER of the Cape Ann National Bank, Glou-
cester, Massachusetts, is an occasional contributor to the
Poet's Column of *The Independent,* and other popular
papers.   He kindly furnishes the two following poems
for the Scrap-Book :

A SUMMER MOOD.

I lay me in the growing grass,
    A vagrant loving vagrancy ;
About me kindred fellows throng,
    A very reckless company.

Gay people of the crowded air,
    Who follow Joy's recruiting drums ;
Nor thrift, nor any thorn—they leave
    To-morrow till to-morrow comes.

Who gathers all, would gather more ;
    Who little hath, hath need of none ;
Who wins a race will long to win
    Another that is never won.

I fling me in the grass, content
    That not a blade belongs to me ;
And take no thought for mowing days—
    A vagrant wed to vagrancy.

WHAT THE SEA WOULD SAY.

The sea comes up by night,
  And comes again by day ;
Through storm and shine it comes
  And looks, then goes away,—

As it doth seek some ear
  To pour a tale upon ;
It comes and comes, and waits
  A moment, and is gone,—

As it doth wait some one
  To stand upon the shore,
That it may tell the tale—
  Then go and come no more.

But generations come
  And generations go ;
The sea knows what it knows,
  And they know what they know.

And what they need they have
  Until they have no need ;
Gold goes from hoard to hand,
  And heirs to heirs succeed.

But the unresting sea
  Hath neither kith nor kin,
Though it must reap and reap,
  And, careless, gather in.

O heart ! hadst thou to beat
  And hope, and earn or win,

Without a heart to share
  What thou hast gathered in !

O sea ! methinks I know
  What thou hast left unsaid,—
'Tis, " Lord, O let me rest ;
  Let me give up my dead !"

HIRAM RICH.

THE two following poems are from the pen of an American cashier, whose modesty requests no further mention :

TO MY ABSENT WIFE.

I have no hopes that are not richly freighted
  With sweetest thoughts of thee ;
I have no wishes but are ever mated
  With such as thine would be.

I breathe no prayer that is not always given
  More for thyself than me ;
I ne'er have sought or aimed, desired or striven,
  But for what both should be.

In dreams I see thee, ever sweet and dear,
  All that my soul desires,
A lovely vision—but to disappear,
  As a dim flame expires.

With thee, my spirit soars to drink and breathe
  Thy purer atmosphere,

And inspirations catch that make, and leave
    Me better, that thou wert here.

It seems to me thou hast no counterpart,
    In any land, to be
Enough to fill my idolizing heart,
    Should'st thou be lost to me.

May Heaven's choicest blessings on thee fall,
    Like dews on sweetest flower ;
Delight and pleasure ever join, to call,
    Thee to their loveliest bower.

Oh ! may contentment be thy lot each day,
    By night, thy pillow be
Sweet peace, whereon thy peerless head to lay,
    And dream sweet dreams of me.
                         B. F. C.

TO ———.

I sit beside my open casement, where,
    Laden with the sweet breath of dewy flowers,
The perfumed winds to my rapt senses bear
    The hush and silence of the midnight hours ;

Hours that grow brighter as the full-robed moon
    Mounts to her zenith ; and, whilst ling'ring there,
Silence sinks into solitude, and the noon
    Of midnight sits upon the voiceless air.

The air itself is hushed and lifeless, and
    Its last, expiring breathings touch my face,
As jeweled fingers of a snowy hand
    Touch delicate petals, or a tender place.

Around me all is dumb and motionless,
　And garish with silv'ry light ; within my heart
Wells up sweet memories, and tries to guess
　Of thee, thy future, and where *now* thou art.

If, too, thou'rt keeping vigils at this hour,
　And sending forth thy thoughts this holy night,
To find and bless, with some invisible power,
　The friends that greet thee with the morning light—

Let *one* swift, white-winged messenger fly here,
　And fold his pinions up, and stay with me,
Till sweet, inviting sleep approaches near,
　When all thy tenants hurry home to thee.

Or art thou in the fairy realm of dreams,
　Reclined in attitudes of sweet repose ?
Whilst the pale moon, like a sweet mother, seems
　To stop, and bend o'er thee, then softly goes

Away so silently, that not a sound
　Springs from her tip-toe movements o'er the floor,
As she pursues her loving vigils round
　The sleeping earth, to watch forevermore.

Oh ! peaceful be thy slumbers, sweet thy dreams,
　May Heavenly visitants thy couch attend,
To guard and keep thee, till the golden beams
　Of morning sunshine on thy head descend !

August, 1878.　　　　　　　　　　B. F. C.

The same statement as to modesty applies to the cashier who furnishes the two following :

BIRTHDAY THOUGHTS.

[ADDRESSED TO MY DEAR WIFE, MAY 2, 1873.]

Another waymark on the journey to Heaven
  Passed by my " Nearest and Dearest " to-day ;
What can I offer her ? what shall be given,
  Joy to afford her on life's thorny way ?

Not all the gems from the depths of the ocean
  Equal in value the treasure I'll bring ;
Believe me, dear Fannie, the heart's fond emotion
  Ever excels e'en what poets can sing.

What though our days seem all laden with sorrow,
  Life-plans and prospects turned rudely aside ;
Faith bids us hope for a brighter to-morrow,—
  Sing, and take courage,—" The Lord will provide !"

Count o'er the blessings our days are revealing,
  "New every morning," unnumbered and free :
Shall we not thankfully, rev'rently kneeling,
  Praise his great *mercies* to you—and to me?

Then let the future bring sorrow or pleasure,
  Bravely we'll meet it, come whatever may ;
Hand joined in hand we'll accept its full measure,
  Fainting nor doubting till life's latest day.

God bless you, my darling ! and grant you whatever
  Infinite wisdom or love can bestow !
Heaven's brightest blessings reward you forever,
  When these dark shadows are ended below !   P.

A PRAYER.

Father of Light ! to Thee I cry,
   Ere yet the day of life be spent !
Hast Thou not said e'en such as I
   Forgiveness find, if penitent ?

" *Nothing but leaves* " my life has borne,—
   Sadness and shame my portion are ;
O'er grievous falls and sins I mourn,
   Which from my God have led me far.

My inward soul for virtue yearns,
   But oh ! the flesh is weak and frail ;
And while tow'rd life my spirit turns,
   Deceitful sins so oft prevail !

A trembling sinner, Lord, I come,
   Owning my wretchedness and woe ;
Before thy righteous throne stand dumb,—
   And shall I unforgiven go ?

Thou who dost for the sparrow care,
   And every creature's record scan,
Oh, hear my deep, repentant prayer,
   Thy mercy show to erring man.

Help me to trust thy promised word,
   To cast on Thee each burd'ning care ;
"Amazing grace" again afford,—
   Let me thy gracious pardon share.

Then, till this fleeting life be past,
   Shall all its powers to Thee be giv'n,
And while eternity shall last,
   ·My soul shall sing thy praise in Heav'n.
  July 25, 1872.   P.

THE BALLAD OF THE ECONOMICAL YOUNG MAN.

[A very lamentable tale, founded on a recent sketch in the *Evening Post.*]

'Tis of a rich Bankier I shall tell you to-day,
Who a Savings Bank Clerk had for his *protegé*,
Twelve hundred a year was his salary all told,
Which the same was paid to him in greenbacks—not gold.
        CHORUS [indicative of the inadequate character
           of his remuneration] :
Singing, tooral, li looral, li looral, li lee,
The greatest of virtues it is economee ;
Take care of the nickels and small currency,
And the dollars'll take care of themselves, don't you
    see?

As the Clerk was walking down Wall Street one day,
He met the rich Bankier, and to him did say :
"Please go to our directors without any delay,
And see if you can't get me a raise in my pay!"
        CHORUS [expressive of his anxiety to have the
           volume of currency made equal to the de-
           mands of his pocket] : Singing, tooral, &c.

" Twelve hundred I have, what I want is fifteen."
Said the Bankier (a man of respectable mien,
With a shaved double chin and gold glasses severe) :
" H—m ! How much do you save of your twelve hun-
    dred a year ?"
        CHORUS [illustrative of the great moral and
           economic truth that 1d. saved is 2d. earned] :
           Singing, tooral, li looral, &c.

"Save? Nothing !" replied that young clerk ; "don't
    you see,
I've a wife and two children all in my familee,

I must house them and clothe them, find them something to eat,
And the best I can do is to make both ends meet."
      CHORUS [descriptive of his struggle for exist-
          ence] : Singing, tooral, li looral, &c.

"Save nothing ?" said sternly that Bankier so good ;
"You may and can save, and might, could, would and
   should.
There's nothing so easy when you're used to it once ;
Now go and come back at the end of six *monce.*"
      CHORUS [conveying the assurance that to him
          that hath shall perhaps be given] : Singing,
          tooral, &c.

That young man went off ; for the next six months he
Did practice the rigidest economee,
He rode to the office each day on shanks' mare,
Losing ten cents' worth of time to save five cents car-fare.
      CHORUS [showing how the old thing worked] :
          Singing, tooral, &c.

With the five cents thus saved he'd repair at high noon
To a beer hall near by, where he'd order a schoon-
Er of lager and sweep the free lunch counter bare,
Of mustard, tripe, sausage, and all that was there.
      CHORUS [pursuing the same theme] : Singing,
          tooral, &c.

When out with the boys a retreat he would beat
As soon as it came near his turn to stand treat,
And when he went to church and the plate was passed round
How meekly he'd fasten his eyes on the ground !
      CHORUS [presenting the fact that salvation is
          to be had without money and without price] :
          Singing, tooral, li looral, &c.

At home his two children this beatified bilk
Paid five cents a day to drink water 'stead of milk,
And when they were asleep the two nickels he'd hook
   'em,
And next morning pretend that the cat 'twas that took
   'em.
      CHORUS [portraying the perfect confidence that
          existed between parent and child] : Sing-
          ing, tooral, &c.

Now, when the appointed six months had passed away,
The Clerk met the Bankier, and to him did say :
" Thanks to the attention to your counsel I did pay,
I've put by two hundred dollars for the next rainy day."
      CHORUS [depicting him as on the high road to
          fortune] : Singing, tooral, li looral, &c.

" Take this note," said the Bankier, "to thy president, he
Will thy salary raise, for good W. E. D.,
When the widows their mites bring to the treasury
Will, I know, not refuse a small whack-up to thee."
      CHORUS [displaying the banker's generosity
          with the money of unsuspecting deposit-
          ors] : Singing, tooral, &c.

At the end of the year, down on Wall Street one day,
The Clerk met the Bankier, and to him did say :
" I've got nine hundred dollars put safely away,
Can you recommend any investment that will pay ?"
      CHORUS [representing the young man as pre-
          pared to take a little flyer] : Singing, too-
          ral, li looral, &c.

Said that Bankier good : "I am one of a pool
Bearing W. U., and I don't think that you'll

For your savings a better investment e'er see
Than to sell a lot short at about 53."   (Chord.)
> CHORUS [describing the disinterested manner in
>   which the good banker gave him points]:
>   Singing, tooral, li looral, &c.

But I grieve to relate at the close of my song,
While the young man went short the Bankier was long,
And when W. U. got to 64, that
The good Bankier unloaded and busted him flat !
> (Slow Curtain.)
> CHORUS [emphasizing the proverb, that " Virtue
>   is its own reward "] :
> Singing, tooral, li looral, li looral, li lee,
> The greatest of virtues it is economee ;
> Take care of the nickels and small currency,
> And the dollars 'll take care of themselves, don't you
>   see ?

NEW YORK, *June*, 1876.   G. T. L.
                              —New York Evening Post.

BANK LOGIC.

Of offenses most rank
Which imperil a Bank,
There is naught like the crime of abstracting ;
Hence the pious cashier
Gets up on his ear
And denounces, with vim most distracting,
The felonious clerk,
Who *adds* to his work,
And *multiplies* sin by *subtracting*

A WALL STREET INCIDENT.

A Tight Money Market. The Bears have it.

The cash from the till
His own pockets to fill,
Until, agonies dreadful protracting;
It is found, all the while
The cashier's private pile
Has been doubled—Bank assets contracting.

So wags the gay world—
Thus the bright top is twirled—
The poor sinner who filches a cracker,
Is damned by the just,
As most false to his trust,
Whilst his judges have characters blacker :
And the pious cashier,
Who for many a year
Made a boast of his high reputation,
Is found out at last
To have muchly surpassed
The meek teller—in crook'd computation.

Indignant Observer.

The above touching lines come from the accomplished Receiver of a certain bank, whose unfortunate affairs he is regulating.

THIS OLD STEEL PEN.

[WRITTEN ABOUT A PEN IN THE DEPOSIT NAT. BANK, DEPOSIT, N. Y.]

I know not when
This aged pen
Began its scribbling race ;

8

I've sought in vain,
Time and again,
To fix both time and place.

I've traveled back
Its tottering track,
For years some half a score ;
And make no doubt
It first set out
As many years before.

Endowed were I
With prophesy,
To light the future plan,
I'd throw a ray,
Adown the way
Through which its pathway ran.

I'd bring to light,
For present sight,
And pattern for to-day,
The fogy ways,
And by-gone days
Of old Methuselah.

Now aged grown,
And staid, I own,
Withal 'tis sharp and quick ;
'Twill shyly hug
This matron mug,
Then dance and jump and kick.

A sober dance,
A Shaker prance,
One not of sin or pride :

And sage may hug
This matron mug
As bridegroom hugs his bride.

And such they are,
An old-time pair,
Contented, faithful, true;
They have their fun,
And sure no one
Will blame them if they do.

For not a day,
In fun or play,
This pen for years hath lost:
Early and late,
To fix your fate,
'Tis faithful at its post.

Your hopes, your fears,
Your joys, your tears,
Exalted or repressed;
Need but invoke
Its ready stroke,
And—you may guess the rest.

Your note or bill,
With ready skill,
'Twill back, accept or sign,
And "Sesame,"
You have the key
To open yonder mine.

To enter there
Be this your care,
The door leave open wide,

For it may be
The self-same key
Won't fit the other side.

Nor ever think
To get the chink ;
For that, with other ills,
Is with those times
When fools made rhymes,
And pens were made of quills.

But what is this ?
Is aught amiss,
Or was I dreaming quite ?
I thought I heard
A grumbling word—
Some words of hate or spite.

" With all my might,
I tried to write
With this confounded pen ;
My paper tore,
I almost swore
I'd never try again.

" Time and again,
I've tried in vain
To make a single letter ;
Then do, I pray,
Take this away,
And let me have a better."

Now I'm awake,
I can't mistake,
I'm sure it was no fable ;

But I protest,
Let this request
Be laid upon the table.

Or, I'll amend,
And to that end
The proposition vary ;
Bring on the new
The work to do,
Let this be—honorary.

December, 1869. T. MORE.

THE TELLER'S SONG OF THE BANK.

Work, work, work !
And stand at the desk all the day ;
Work, work, work !
And bid an adieu to all play ;
Work, and be constantly driven ;
Wear the flesh from your bones and your face ;
The outsiders think banking is Heaven,
But it's more like the opposite place !

Count, count, and write !
Count money all day long ;
And on taking your balance at night,
Have the cash come provokingly wrong ;
Then look till you're nervous and cross,
And hunt till you almost fear
You must charge it to Profit and Loss,
And at last—*find it on the Cashier !*

Post, and compare, and post !
Post, and compare, and check !

And work till you are almost
  Of your former self a wreck.
Post, and check, and compare,
  Check, and compare, and foot,
Till you're driven almost to despair,
  By the work which upon you is put.

Ledger and Journal and Cash,
  And Blotter and Register too,
And the whole of that blue-edged trash,
  Which it take one so long to write through.
I wish they could all be turned back
  To rags, real dirty and rank;
And be stuffed down the mouth of that jack
  Who first invented a bank.

From *The Hartford Times*, Conn., 1852.

HOW TO GET RICH.

If you will take a bank-note, and, while folding it up according to direction, peruse the following lines, you will arrive at their meaning, with no little admiration for the writer's cleverness:

"I will tell you a plan for gaining wealth,
  Better than banking, trading or leases;
Take a bank-note and fold it up,
  And then you will find your wealth in-creases.

"This wonderful plan, without danger or loss,
  Keeps your cash in your hands, and with nothing to
    trouble it;
And every time that you fold it across,
  'Tis plain as the light of the day that you double it."

A Banking office in Connecticut, dealing in Arizona Mining Stocks, has a genius who has produced the following :

SILVER JINGLE.

Dig miners, dig—dig with care
The precious treasure in the Ar-
Izona mines of bright silvaire ;
Buy, neighbors, buy the tempting share
Of the precious treasure in the Ar-
Izona mines of bright silvaire.

Ten hundred per cent. in the gold ore fair,
Ten hundred per cent. in the silver rare,
Ten hundred per cent. in the rich coppaire,
A thousand per cent. for each dollaire,
To fill the pockets of the customaire.
Buy, neighbors, buy the tempting share,
Till your pockets burst with the bright silvaire.

Come, brothers, come, and take a share
In the silver mine that promises fair
To pay such dividends that you will stare.
You won't find such chances everywhere.
    " Ten hundred per cent. &c."

There are *eleven* verses of the same sort, the machine having got going and couldn't be stopped.

———————•———————

" Accursed Debt ! in whose relentless coils
So many brave souls have been crushed to death :
Thy slimy coils contaminate aught they touch,
Nor let the purest soul escape untarnished !
        God save us from thee !"

THE ANCIENT BOOK-KEEPER.

BY GEORGE COOPER.

It was an ancient book-keeper,
  And he was tall and slim ;
Tho' his face was mild, he rarely smiled ;
  His clothes were dark and prim,
And everything about his desk
  He kept exceeding trim.

He always hung his hat and coat
  Upon the self-same hooks,
And laid his ruler, pen and ink
  In their respective nooks,
And the only exercise he had
  Was footing up his books.

Each day, upon the self-same hour,
  He took his lofty seat,
And bent his body and his mind,
  His labors to complete ;
And blots were neither on his fame,
  Nor on his ledger sheet.

The music of his pen was heard
  From morn till eventide ;
Up columns vast his eyes were cast,
  Then down again with pride ;
Quite pleased was he, though he saw his work
  Increased and multiplied.

The cash that o'er his fingers came
  Each day, was something grand ;

And yet no schemes to bear it off
  By him were ever planned ;
Although you saw with half an eye
  That he wrote a "sloping" hand.

He had no wife, he made no friends,
  His joys and cares were few ;
And his dearest hope from day to day
  Was to keep his balance true ;
A good world this, if every man
  The latter thing would do.

He never sighed when little ills
  His way of life would cross ;
And o'er the errors of his youth
  He showed no vain remorse ;
But set down all that came along
  To profit or to loss.

One day the Creditor of all
  Dropped in for his amount ;
He found the old man at his post,
  Though low ran nature's fount ;
The books were closed, and he was borne
  Up to his last account.

A MONODY ON MONEY.

[DEDICATED TO OUR "VERY" PARTICULAR BANKERS.]

"I know a bank " where busy men are daily seen to
  pore
Over their books, with earnest zeal, from ten o'clock till
  four;

8*

From whose retreat are issued forth more rich and
    treasured notes
Than ever have been known to come from sweetest song-
    birds' throats ;
Where crowns abound and sov'reigns rule the place
    with despot sway,
For no one there will check their power, so well belov'd
    are they.
There seems a money mania for everything that's dear,
And, strange as it may seem, I've heard that far-things
    here are near.
Cleopatra drank pearls, they say, but here she is
    outvied—
If pork they wish they've guinea pigs ; if beef, the silver
    side.
Their drink is pure aqua d'ora, and I have heard it's
    true
Their servant men are Bills and Franks, their house-
    maid is a Sou.
And now, before I end my lay, I ought to make it
    known
That though this bank is always thronged, each one
    may get a-loan ;
And though these bankers care for gold, it never can be
    said
Matter-o-money it will be if ever they are wed.

[FOUND WRITTEN IN LADIES' SCRIPT, ON AN OLD BANK NOTE.]

Well might the immortal Shakespeare say 'twere trash,
If then, as now, men dealt in paper cash.

MOTHER GOOSE IN WALL STREET.

Hark ! hark ! the banks do bark,
  The brokers have come to town,
Some with bags and some with rags,
  To hunt the specie down.

_____

There was a man in our town,
  Who was so wondrous wise
He jumped into a first-class bank
  And drew out his supplies;
And when he got his money out,
  With all his might and main,
He rushed into another bank,
    And concluded that, all things considered, he
      might as well deposit it again.

_____

Here we go, up, up, up,
  Here we go, round, round, roundy,
Here we go, backward and forward,
  Here we go, down, down, downy.
                         (*Stock Reports.*)

_____

Note-shaver ! note-shaver !
    Fly away home !
  Your notes are protested,
    Your fingers will burn.

_____

Baa ! baa ! bank-sheep, have you any gold ?
  Yes, marry have I, three bags told ;
One for depositors, one for me,
  And one for an old chap that lives across the sea.

Buy my check, pay my check, banker's man.
No, I can't, master, by any plan.
Then take it and cross it and mark it with **G**,
And then it will do for "Smithy" and me.

———

High ding diddle, remember Nick Biddle,
 The banks have gone up like balloons ;
The Democrats laughed to see the sport,
 And Ben ran away with the spoons !

———

Pretty Director ! your bank let me milk,
I'll give your lady an imported silk,
And a dozen gloves, as you shall see,
If you will come down with a discount to me.

———

AFTER BURNS.

'Tis naught when woman humbugs man,
 For that's the good old style ;
But oh, man's confidence in man
 Makes countless thousands smile.

———◆———

THE POPULAR CREED—DIMES AND DOLLARS.

Dimes and dollars, dollars and dimes !
An empty pocket is the worst of crimes !
If a man's down give him a thrust—
Trample the beggar into the dust !
Presumptuous poverty is quite appalling—
Knock him over ! kick him for falling !

If a man's up, oh ! lift him higher !
Your soul's for sale, and he's the buyer.

    Dimes and dollars, dollars and dimes !
    An empty pocket is the worst of crimes.

I know a bold and honest man,
Who strives to live on the Christian's plan,
But poor he is, and poor will be,
A scorned and hated wretch is he ;
At home he meeteth a starving wife,
Abroad he leadeth a leper's life.
They struggle against a fearful odds
Who will not bow to the people's gods !

    Dimes and dollars, dollars and dimes !
    An empty pocket is the worst of crimes !

I know a poor but worthy youth,
Whose hopes are built on a maiden's truth ;
But the maiden will break her vow with ease,
For a wooer cometh whose charms are these :
A hollow heart and an empty head,
A nose well tinged with brandy red,
A soul well trained in villainy's school—
But cash, sweet cash—he knoweth the rule :

    Dimes and dollars, dollars and dimes !
    An empty pocket is the worst of crimes !

So get ye wealth, no matter how !
" No questions asked " of the rich, I trow !
Steal by night and steal by day
(Doing it all in a legal way) ;
Join the church and never forsake her ;
Learn to cant and insult your Maker ;

Be hypocrite, liar, knave and fool,
But don't be poor ; remember the rule :

Dimes and dollars, dollars and dimes !
An empty pocket is the worst of crimes !
By one of the Immortal Unknown.

ON A POSTAL CARD.

Blessings be on thee and on thy designer,
  Thou little penny parallelogram ;
And, if thou art in every sense its minor,
  I like thee better than the telegram.

Thou art less swift and, happily, less stealthy,—
  Not gliding on us like a midnight ghost.
I leave the wires for the fast and wealthy,
  And sing thy virtues, little penny-post.

There is no air of secrecy about thee,
  Thou comest on the square, with open face ;
And half the world were at a loss, without thee,
  To get and send much news in little space.

Thy cheapness is but one of virtues many,
  Thou art, besides, a labor-saving plan ;
It costs us but a pen-scratch and a penny
  To write to Dick—" or any other man."

I only hope 'twill not become the fashion
  (I hear with pain the process has begun)
To mar thy face by sending claims for cash on,
  For then, alas ! thy wit and worth are *dun.*

But may thy open face rebuke all evil,
  And check all malice of the pen and press.

The sealed envelope better suits the D——l
To cover schemes of wrong and wantonness.
W. C. Richards.

———————

Watts, adapted to the requirements of a certain note-shaver.

"Blest be that man whose sole intent
 Is righteously to live.
A pious heart and twelve per cent.
 Makes all that life can give."

———————

A CASUS ANATOMICUS.

A wealthy banker died ; his body was dissected ;
No symptom of disease was anywhere detected
Until they reached the heart—to find they were unable,
But in the place was found—a compound interest table !

———————

A Mechanicsburg, Pa., bank once paid a check on which some spirituous-ly inclined poet had indorsed :

"The melancholy days have come,—
 The saddest of the year ;
Not cold enough for whisky punch,—
 I'll invest this V in beer.'

———————

When panics come, who seems to wear
A calm, serene, superior air,
As though it wasn't his affair ?
My broker !
—London Charivari.

A HINT TO YOUNG MEN.

"Only a name to be written down here—
A name not my own ; how I tremble with fear !
One dash of the pen, up and down strokes say twenty,
And the bold deed is done that will bring me cash
    plenty.
The strong man (?) determines, then falters with dread,
While the simple word 'only' runs wild through his
    head,
Ay, only an act, done in ten seconds' time—
Only a forgery—only a crime !

"Only a cell, with its limited space—
Only black ruin and blacker disgrace ;
Forfeited honor and standing and truth ;
Primitive cause—too much license in youth.
Only a penny, and only a dime ;
Only a dollar or two to kill time ;
Only—till no earthly power can save ;
Only till left—there is only the grave."

A broker sends a New York paper his addition to the
Litany in this feeling style :

"From Chapman's Iron Mountain,
    From Stockwell's A. and P. ;
From Western Union's Divvy,
    From Boston, H. & E. ;
From Jay Gould's North-West Corner,
    From Dick Schell's Guaranty—
From all these Wall street bubbles
    Good Lord, deliver me !"

The following lines have been printed on the back of many of the " Gray-backs," or Confederate bills, which circulated so extensively in the Southern States during the late war. They were written by Major S. A. Jonas, of the Texas Brigade:

"IN MEMORIAM.

["RESPECTFULLY DEDICATED TO THE HOLDERS OF CONFEDERATE
TREASURY NOTES.]

" Representing nothing on God's earth now,
    And nought in the waters below it,
  As a pledge of the nation that's dead and gone,
    Keep it, dear friend, and show it.

"Too poor to possess the precious ores,
    And too much of a stranger to borrow,
  We issued to-day our promise to pay,
    And hoped to redeem on the morrow.

"The days rolled on and weeks became years,
    But our coffers were empty still ;
  Coin was so rare that the Treasury quaked,
    If a dollar should drop in the till.

" We knew it had hardly a value in gold,
    Yet as gold our soldiers received it ;
  It gazed in our eyes with a promise to pay,
    And each patriot soldier believed it.

" Keep it, for it tells our history all o'er,
    From the birth of its dream to the last ;
  Modest, and born of the angel Hope,
    Like the hope of success—it *passed*."

A NEW INDUSTRY.

The great economic question of the day,
Labor, is solved in a way .
                    That is no joke. .
North and South, industrial schools,
All, should know the rules
                    For disposing of smoke.
In your chimneys put ladders—
Get balloons, baskets and bladders—
                    And carry it out—
Thus you give the students a show,
To pay up as they go,
                    And to keep off the gout.
Never mind about the faces :
To red and black races
                    It is well suited.
And, I dare say, for the white
It will prove just right—
                    If not refuted. .

(PRIVATE.—To the Scrap-Book.)

You may think it foolish,
To put anything schoolish
                    In these pages ;
But if on *selling* you're bent,
You must give equivalent
                    the sages.

                              CROWELL.

The above, from the ready pen and pencil of a "Boss
Printer" in an industrial school not far from Hampton,

Va., where a new workshop with tall chimney is going up, and where little Indians and young Africans are taught how to labor and to learn, has perhaps but mild reference to the bank business, though it may illustrate some moral point in stock-bubble operations. It will bear close study, and being a long way ahead of some other things pasted in this Scrap-Book, it has a right to its little page.

———◆———

" This world is the best, that we
   live in,
   To lend, or to spend, or to give
   in ;
   But to beg, or to borrow, or get
   a man's own,
   'Tis the very worst world, sir,
   that ever was known."
                    OLD SONG.

A NEW INDUSTRY.

———◆———

The finance-minister, under whose reign England was fated to become for a time an irredeemable-paper-money

country, was thus satirized in a current epigram of the
day :

"Of Augustus and Rome
  The poets still warble;
How he found it of brick,
  And left it of marble.
So of Pitt and of England
  We may say without vapor,
That he found it of gold,
  And left it of paper."

------·------

CRŒSUS.

My little Charlie said to me
  That he had lots of riches.
"How much, old man?" said I ; said he,
  "Two farthings in my breeches,

"A silver fourpence in my purse,
  And one French bit of money,"
Then added (speaking of his nurse),
  "'Twas given me by Nunny.

"A lucky sixpence, father, too ;"
  He paused as though to measure
With those grave eyes what I should do,
  On hearing of such treasure.

With those grave eyes he looked at me,
  Ere he resumed his parley—
It was as plain as A, B, C,
  (Or plainer, perhaps, to Charlie),

That weighty matters were our cue,
  We meant to sift and try 'em—

"And father," Charlie said, "are you
  As rich a man as I am?"

And I replied—the while I drew
  My arm around his shoulder—
"Charlie, I'm not so rich as you,
  Because I'm ages older."
                    —*London Spectator.*

————♦————

GOLD.

If hoarded gold possessed the power
To lengthen life's too fleeting hour,
And purchase from the hand of Death
A little span, a moment's breath,
How I would love the precious ore,
And every hour should swell my store;
That when Death came with shadowy pinion,
To waft me to his bleak dominion,
I might by bribes my doom delay,
And bid him call some distant day.
But since not all earth's golden store
Can buy for us one bright hour more,
Why should we vainly mourn our fate,
Or sigh at life's uncertain date?
Nor wealth nor grandeur can illume
The silent midnight of the tomb.
No—give to others hoarded treasures—
Mine be the brilliant round of pleasures;
The goblet rich, the board of friends,
Whose social souls the goblet mends;
And mine, while yet I've life to live,
Those joys that love alone can give.
                —*Moore's Odes of Anacreon.*

YOUTH AND AGE.

How slow, how sure, how swift,
  The sands within each glass,
  The brief illusive moments pass !
Half unawares we mark their drift,
  Till the awakened heart cries out,—Alas !
Alas, the fair occasion fled,
The precious chance to action all unwed !
And murmurs in its depths the old refrain,—
Had we but known betimes what now we know in vain !

When the vail from the eyes is lifted,
  The seer's head is gray ;
When the sailor to shore has drifted
  The sirens are far away.
Why must the clearer vision,
  The wisdom of Life's late hour,
Come, as in Fate's derision,
  When the hand hath lost its power?

Is there a rarer being,
  Is there a fairer sphere,
Where the strong are not unseeing,
  And the harvests are not sere ;
Where, ere the seasons dwindle
  They yield their due return ;
Where the lamps of knowledge kindle,
  While the flames of youth still burn ?
Oh, for the young man's chances !
  Oh, for the old man's will !
Those flee while this advances,
  And the strong years cheat us still.
                —*Stedman's Dartmouth Ode.*

HUMOROUS CLIPPINGS AND LAUGH-ABLE EXPERIENCES.

"I am persuaded that every time a man smiles—but much more so when he laughs—it adds something to this fragment of life."
—STERNE.

"Every time a man laffs he takes a kink out ov the chain ov life, and thus lengthens it."—BILLINGS.

HUMOR OF CASHIERS' NAMES.

IN the Cashier's Directory of the United States, the reader can readily learn "what's in a name," and will doubtless be amused and edified to know how many bear so appropriate and suggestive a cognomen. We cull the following specimens :

There are 2 Angells, 1 Raphael, 1 Batt, 4 Cranes, 1 Kite, 2 Rich men and 1 Poor man ; 2 Shoemakers and 1 Squire ; 1 Pope, 1 Church, 4 Bishops and 2 Temples ; 2 Mills and 15 Millers ; 2 Little men, 2 Long and 1 Low man ; a Mr. Sharp, Mr. Quirk (presumably a lawyer), Mr. Flint, Mr. Fogg, Mr. Bird, Mr. Doe (not John) and Mr. Drake. There is 1 Early man, 4 Fisher men, 1 Fidlar, 2 Colliers, 7 Cooks, 4 Carpenters, 2 Nobles, 4 Kings, besides *Miss Annie M. King* (cashier at New Sharon, Iowa), 2 descendants of Ham, 5 Greens, 2 Gold-

[71]

smiths, 1 Glazier, 2 Gay fellows, 4 Lambs, 1 Buck, 2 Lepper, 8 Bells, 1 Chick and 1 Child, and one man who is certainly a *Dame.* One cashier is a Jack, another a Good-sell, and still another remarkably Sweet. But we grieve to say there are 3 who are Skinners! 4 whose *names*, at least, are Steel! (to spare their feelings we spell it the other way), and there are but 1 Manly person, 2 Learned men, and 1 Just man reported in the entire lot. Imagine all these standing in line for dress parade! "PER SE."

QUEER BANK TITLES.

Niedersaechsische Bank.
Deutsche Genossenschafts Bank.
Braunschweigische Bank.
Schaafhausencher Bank Verien.
Bayerische Hypotheken und Wechsel Bank.
Mecklenburgische Hypotheken und Wechsel Bank.
(Not necessary to say the above are in Germany.)

In the Netherlands, we find :
The Commanditaire Bankvereeniging.

In Sweden :
Skandinaviska Kredit Aktie Bolaget, and Aktiebolaget Göteborg Köpmannss Bank.

In Hungary :
Filiale der Oesterreichischen Credit-Anstalt.

And the Wise Men of Athens bank their savings in the

Banque Hellénique de Crédit Général.

It is hoped these institutions are well provided with printed forms, address-cards, &c.,—as life is short.

————◆————

WORKING BOTH WAYS.

A number of very smart bank-clerks have drawn up the rules for customers which we print below, and have amused themselves and insulted the public by display-ing these rules over the bank counters. They are poor rules which will not work both ways ; and we therefore add to them a few rules for clerks, and print the two sets of instructions in parallel columns, so that he who runs may read. In this form they will be found suitable for any bank, and we hope to see them pasted all over the country.

We have only to add that there would be more necessity for our rules if the majority of bank-clerks had not adopted them in practice already.

RULES FOR BANK CUSTOMERS.	RULES FOR BANK CLERKS.
1. If you have any business with a bank put it off until three o'clock, or, if possible, a little later,	1. Always remember that the bank is open for your own convenience—not for the use of its patrons—

4

as it looks more business-like to rush in as the bank is closing.

2. Never put stamps on your checks before you get to the bank, but give the teller two cents, and ask him to lick it and cancel it for you ; the teller expects to lick all the stamps, and it is a source of disappoint-ment to him when people insist on doing it them-selves, and will save him buying his lunch.

3. It is best not to take your bank book with you, but call at another time and have it entered. You can thus make two trips to the bank where one would answer.

4. If a check is made payable to your order, be careful not to indorse it before handing it to the teller, but let him return it to you and wait while you indorse it ; this helps to pass the time, and is a

and govern yourselves ac-cordingly.

2. Make all the fuss you can about stamps. Say you haven't any, or can't sell them. Give the customer as much trouble as possible

3. In paying checks always give out the largest bills. Customers are so fond of $100 bills.

4. Always grumble very loudly about making up the bank-books. What right has a customer to know how his account stands?

pleasure and relief to the teller. You can generally save time when making a deposit by counting down your money to the teller, as you can nearly always count more speedily and correctly than he can.

5. If you make a deposit of $100 and give a check for $50, it is a good thing to call frequently at the bank and ask how your account stands, as it impresses the officers favorably with your business qualifications.

6. When your notes come due and payment is requested, ask why they can't wait, and what they intend to do with the money when they get it. If they still persist, inquire if the bank is hard up, that they should be in such want for money. Never pay protest fees, but say you forgot when this note matured, and that you

5. If you know the indorser of a check, say that you do not know his handwriting. Never pay a check if you can help it. This keeps the money in the bank.

6. In counting money, correct all the mistakes which tell against the bank ; but stick to those which rob the customer.

never pay protest fees any-how,—you would be d—d first.

7. When you present to the bank a draft, payable to your order, never fail to exhibit profound surprise and fierce indignation that you are required to be identified as the proper person to receive the money. If the teller per-sists in this eccentric re-quest, affirm boldly how long you have lived at No. 2244 Brown street, and how Timothy Snobbin has known you all his life. Stand up for your rights like a man, and never say fail.

8. In banking money, spread yourself before the bank counter, and count your shinplasters bottom-side up, one by one, and, showing them to the teller in sundry piles, entertain him meanwhile by a gen-eral report of your private

7. It is the duty of every customer to make a good impression upon you. If he does not, take no notice of him when he wants change or cash.

8. Of course you will never be weak enough to give a customer notice when his notes fall due. Why should you care if he be ruined ?

affairs. In this manner you not only astonish the bank officials with the display of your money, but, by exercising the patience of such nervous customers as may be waiting for their turn, you accomplish a public good.

9. Always date your checks ahead, it is a never-failing sign that you keep a good balance in bank; or, if you do not wish it generally known that you are doing a good business, do not deposit your money until about the time you expect your check will be in.

10. In depositing money never make out a deposit ticket. The teller has the blanks in his case for that purpose, and expects to fill them out himself. It annoys him to have you offer to do it; besides, if others are waiting, it gives them a chance to exercise

9. Recollect that you are not the servant of the bank patrons; but a great man, to whom they should cringe. You must cringe to the president and cashier; but bully the customers to make up for it.

10. If there be a mistake of a date or a figure on a deposit ticket, never correct it. Send the customer back to make out another. His time is of no value, and yours is priceless.

patience, which is a great virtue.

11. In receiving money from a teller, never say in advance how you want it, but hand back each note separately, and ask him to break it.

Banks have high notions, but show them that you know what's what, and don't let them fool you.

A strict observance of the foregoing rules will make your account desirable for any bank, and make you a general favorite with all the bank officers.

11. Scowl at anybody who asks you for currency or change. Why should people bother you about such trifles, when your mighty mind is full of pie or Sarah Ann?

A strict observance of the foregoing rules will make you a desirable clerk, a model of your class, and a favorite with the suffering public.

MISTAKEN IDENTITY.

The genial cashier of the Holton Exchange Bank, Kansas, claims to be "no artist as well as no poet, but the pioneer bank of Jackson County," having started in '72, in a little one-story, one-room *frame* building.

During those early days of frontier financiering, there appeared one day at the counter a couple of Texas rangers, who desired the meek man in waiting to "set

us up a couple o' glasses, Mister." The cashier hesitating, the request was repeated rather emphatically. Per-
ceiving they were in earnest, he asked them at last what
they took him for, and exhibiting a bottle of "Arnold's
Fluid," assured those children of the desert that that was
the only stimulant there dealt in, and persuaded them
he was by no means running a saloon. They left.

A COMMON INCIDENT.

Enter, a positive customer. He desires to deposit a
hundred dollars. Cashier makes it but seventy-six.

"I put down a *hundred*, sir! I'll take my *affidavit* I
did, sir!" Blusters about a few minutes, and gets excited over it. At last the old man opens his memoran-
dum-book again, and takes a fresh look. "Ah! here
they are—twenty and two 2's! Beg pardon," &c., &c.

THE MARRYING BANK.

Our five-year-old Richie, who is "peart" and inquisi-
tive, astonished his governor this morning with the query:
"Papa, do they marry people in that Bank?" "Of
course not," is the immediate reply; "what possessed
you to ask that?" "Why, it says 'Marine Bank' over
the door, and why should they put up the sign if they
don't do it?"

First National Bank of Red Bank, N. J., Dec. 12, 1878, sends in its experiences thus:

A check was presented to me by an Irishman, to be cashed, who had not indorsed it. I returned it to him, telling him to put his name on it. When handed to me again, I noticed that he had written his name on the face of the check. I threw it to him, and said, " Across the back ;" when handed me the third time, it was with the remark—"Seems to me you fellows are divilish particular," and with a large cross roughly drawn on the back.

An Irishman, unknown to me, presented a check of one of our customers, payable to the order of Pat O'Flaherty. I told him it would be necessary for him to bring some one to identify him. " Identify ! and what in God's name is that ?" he answered. I endeavored to explain to him that he must go and bring in some of his friends whom we knew to satisfy us that he was Pat O'Flaherty. " All right," he said, and started off ; but had scarcely gone fifty yards when he returned, and with a knowing twinkle in his eye, called out to me, "See here, if I'm not Pat O'Flaherty, who the divil am I ?" This was unanswerable.

CHEAP SILVER.

It occurred twenty-two years ago, when I was cashier of a country bank. I had been to the city of ——, to

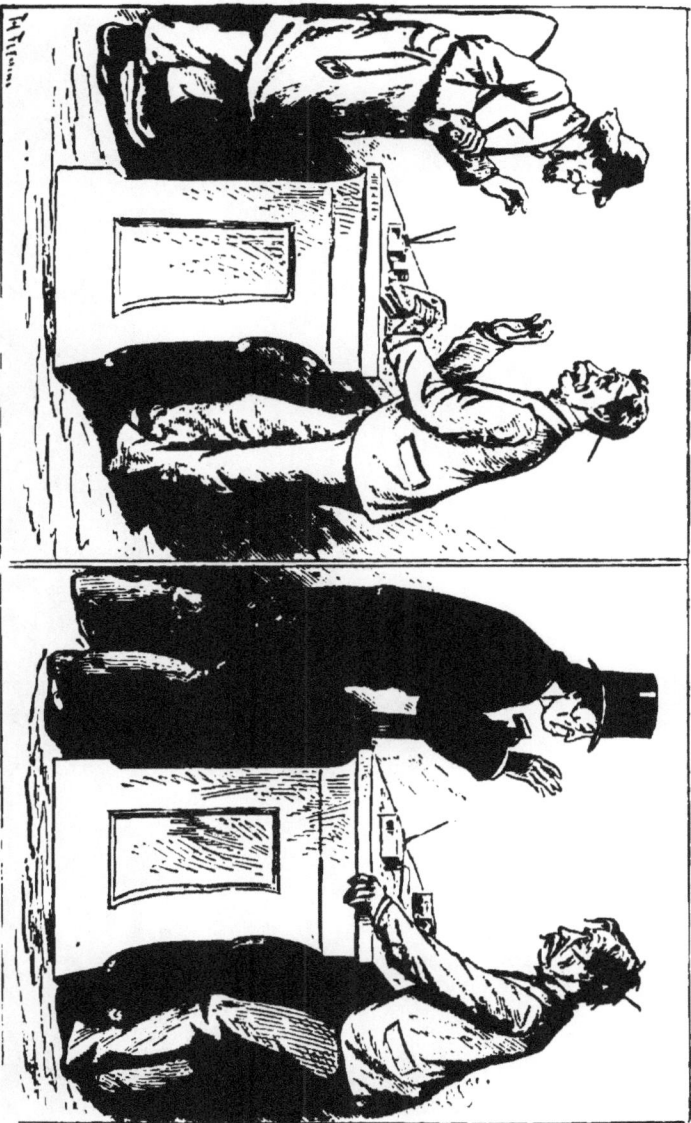

FACIAL EXPRESSION.—"It is rather hard upon the Cashier who is supposed to please all the depositors, to have to laugh at the joke of the facetious customer one moment, and the next to sympathize with one who has lost a relative."—*Cashier Davis, of Cambridgeport, Mass.*

bring home a sum of silver coin for daily use, and whilst I was seated at my table counting and putting it into paper rolls of five and ten dollars each, an old gentleman entered the bank, and his bright eyes soon discovered the great pile of new silver quarters before me. Elated at the sight (for he was a genuine Bentonian Democrat), he quickly asked me where I obtained them. I replied, "At the mint, of course." "Is it possible?" said he; "and what do you have to pay for them?" "Oh," said I, "not much; I can get all I want at the same price I paid for these." "And how much was that?" earnestly questioned he. "Well," I replied, "I got this pile which you see, for *twelve* and *thirteen* cents apiece, and I was offered as much more at the same rates." "You don't say so!" "Yes," I answered, "there's nothing remarkable in that, is there?" "Why, yes; could you get some for me on the same terms, and will you take the trouble to do so for me?" "Certainly," I replied, "and I will give you as many of this *pile* for your present need as you may require." The old gentleman had seldom been away from the shadow of his dwelling and out-buildings on a well-to-do farm away out in the country, and had never read anything but the *Globe* and *Democrat*, but he at once drew his check for all his balance in the bank and handed it to me, with many thanks for my courtesy. I handed over to him its value in silver quarters, but it was some time before he realized that *twelve* and *thirteen* cents were *jointly* necessary to purchase one of Uncle Sam's silver quarters.

B. F. C.

AN IRISH AFFIDAVIT.

Some time in December, 1878, the coal companies in this town paid the miners the wages due them for the preceding month, and, as is the custom throughout the anthracite coal region, the miners gave the pay to their wives. A Mrs. K——, of this place, had received the money from her husband, and left her pocket-book lying on the table in the kitchen, with a portion of a $20 U. S. note sticking out at the clasp. A goat, seeing the green paper, jumped on the table, opened the pocket-book, and before Mrs. K—— had time to look around, the goat had eaten the twenty-dollar note. Mr. K—— immediately killed the goat, and took the chewed-up bill from its entrails. Mrs. K—— came to our institution in great distress, with the mutilated pieces, and we directed her to make an affidavit stating the manner in which the bill was destroyed, so as to have it redeemed by the Treasury Department. She returned the following affidavit, made before an Irish alderman of this place :

State of Penna,
Schuylkill County. } *ss. :*

On this 14th day of December, 1878, before me, a justice of the peace, personally appeared Mrs. Bridget K——, who, being duly sworn according to law, doth depose and say that the twenty-dollar bill now in controversy was taken out of a pocket-book and eaten by a goat, and that said bill was taken out of the body or guts of said goat.

(Sig.)   JOHN O'BRIEN, J. P.

While we did not send the affidavit to Washington, but retained it as a specimen legal document, we prepared another for her, forwarded it to the Treasury Department at Washington, and had the bill redeemed.

W. G., *Teller.*

———◆———

RESPONSIBILITY OF "THE OTHER FELLOW."

In country towns are always found an impecunious few, who, by the regularity with which their notes go to protest, seem to have been created or to live solely for the benefit of the notary public. There is another class, in regard to the object of whose existence there is no question, who are known as the two-per-cent.-a-month brokers. Clearly, these live for themselves. Not long ago, in one of the flourishing cities of the State, a member of the fourth estate, a "local" editor, who had done much in his time for the note-brokers and notaries public, was called upon by one of the former, who held in his hand a protested note of the editor, which, strange to say, was well indorsed. Said he, "Come, I want you to pay this note; what are you going to do about it?"

"Do about it? Nothing. Didn't I have trouble enough about that note on the *go in?* When I get a *good* indorser, my trouble is over; possibly his begins. Go and see the other fellow; don't bother me."

The broker comprehended the scope of the observation, and promenaded for the other party.

THE WISE AND FOOLISH BURGLARS.

[A WORLD FABLE.]

Ten Burglars, five of whom were Wise and five Foolish, having taken their Dark Lanterns, went forth to rob a Bank. The Foolish Burglars toiled assiduously at the Safe with Oxy-hydrogen Blowpipes, Gunpowder and Drills, and had just opened it and made the Discovery that it was Empty when, at midnight, there was a Cry, " Behold, the Police Cometh," and they were made prisoners and sent up for Twenty Years. The Wise Burglars, however, having noticed that the Respectable Cashier of the Bank had recently dyed his Hair and given much thought to the Advertisements of Transatlantic Steamers, broke into his dwelling, where they did not fail to obtain all the Funds and Negotiable Securities of the Institution.

Moral.—" Wall Street Did It All."

----------&----------

"CHATTEL MORTGAGES."

While telling in one of the Western branches of the Exchange Bank of Canada some three or four years ago, I was greatly amused at the following :—One afternoon an old farmer entered the office and asked if he could borrow some money. I, of course, referred him to Mr. Cameron—our manager—who asked him if he could give an indorser. The farmer said he wouldn't ask his *father* to indorse his note, but, if we liked, he would give us a *cattle* mortgage on some good steers and oxen he had at home. This reply caused general laughter among the clerks, and our friend left the office in no very good humor, not being able to understand why the manager should refuse to advance money on such security as a first-class "*Cattle Mortgage.*" H. B. H.

EVERY MAN TO HIS TRADE.

About two weeks ago a couple of countrymen entered our office, in this city, and presented for payment a check of three hundred odd dollars. Being in a hurry, I gave it to him "pretty lively" in fours. One of the fellows, standing with mouth and eyes wide open, evidently took considerable interest in the counting. After I had finished, he asked his friend if he thought he could do it as fast as that? "No," said he, "I'm not much on the count; but I'll bet five dollars that I can beat him hollow feeding a threshing-machine." H. B. H.

London, Ont.

THE PROCRASTINATING BROKER.

A procrastinating broker met a rich but simple cap-italist, who was going down to Wall street with a bag of gold. "To-morrow," he said to himself, "I will unload some Pacific Mail on that snoozer." But, lo! when the morrow came, he found out that the capitalist had gone short on Union Pacific the night before and lost his pile !

Moral.—Never put off till to-morrow the man you can do to-day.—*" Out of the World" Fables.*

SMART BOYS.

It is one of the peculiarities of the child of Indiana, that one of his earliest developments is a genius for finance. At Lafayette, recently, a gentleman who teaches a class in Sunday-school, by way of illustrating a certain point, took from his pocket a new silver dollar, and asked, " What is this?"

A little fellow responded, " Ninety-two cents."

This was not exactly apropos, so the teacher went on: " What is this motto on it ?"

" In God we trust," responded another young numismatist.

" What do we trust him for ?" continued the teacher.

" For the other eight cents," replied the first little financier, and that ended the dialogue.

ROTHSCHILD'S RIDE.

There is a good story told of Baron Rothschild, of Paris, the richest man of his class in the world, which shows that it is not only "money which makes the mare go" (or horses either, for that matter), but "*ready money*," "unlimited credit" to the contrary notwithstanding. On a very wet and disagreeable day, the Baron took a Parisian omnibus on his way to the Bourse, or Exchange, near which the "Nabob of Finance" alighted, and was going away without paying. The driver stopped him and demanded his fare. Rothschild felt in his pocket, but he had not a "red cent" of change. The driver was very wroth:

"Well, what did you get *in* for, if you could not pay? You must have *known* that you had no money!"

"I am Baron Rothschild!" exclaimed the great capitalist; "and there is my card!"

The driver threw the card in the gutter. "Never heard of you before," said he, "and don't want to hear of you again. But I want my fare—and I must *have* it!"

The great banker was in haste. "I have only an order for a million," he said. "Give me the change;" and he proffered a "coupon" for fifty thousand francs.

The conductor stared, and the passengers set up a horse-laugh. Just then an "Agent de Change" came by, and Baron Rothschild borrowed of him the six sous.

The driver was now seized with a kind of remorseful respect; and turning to the money-king, he said: "If you want ten francs, sir, I don't mind lending them to you on my own account."

A KANSAS INCIDENT.

Once upon a time, we called on a man who owed us $25, for payment, and hearing that he had money in a bank in a neighboring city, we asked him for a check for the amount on said bank ; this he gave us willingly (we filling out the check, he signing it). The check went to protest. A few weeks after we met the party, who accosted us as follows : "Vell, dot money vas paid all right. I got mine receipts for de monish." He got his notice of protest !

NOT UPSET.

At the time when Sir John Dean Paul's bank stopped payment, a witty lawyer was met coming out of it by a friend.

"So Sir John has failed?" said the friend.

"Yes," replied the lawyer, "and I've been victimized."

"Really!" continued the other; "the news must have quite upset you."

"Not at all; I was not upset, although I lost my *balance*."

THE MERCHANT OF VENICE.

A Venetian merchant who was lolling in the lap of luxury was accosted upon the Rialto by a friend who had not seen him for many months. "How is this?"

cried the latter; "when I last saw you your gaberdine was out at elbows, and now you sail in your own gondola." "True," replied the merchant, "but, since then I have met with serious losses, and been obliged to compound with my creditors for ten cents on the dollar."

Moral.—Composition is the life of trade.

"Out of the World" Fables.

———————•———————

This,—from Red Oak, Iowa.

HE HAD HIS RECEIPT.

A "granger" who wanted to send forty dollars to an eastern loan company to pay his interest coupon, purchased a draft for that purpose of us the 1st of June last, and when the next coupon had matured and the first one had not been received, he wanted us to write and find out the reason. We did so, and when he came in to-day to find out the cause of delay and we told him that they had never received the money and were just on the point of foreclosing the mortgage, you could have hung your hat on his eyes. "Why, I have your *receipt* for the money," said he ; and going down in his "jeans," he produced an old leather pocket-book, and unrolling it in a manner that would have made Solon Shingle blush, he produced our draft on Chicago issued six months ago. I told the innocent that that was the money, and he should have sent that in his letter. Then there stole over his countenance a sad and sorrowful smile

that smole itself away into a look of unutterable orphan-
age and hopeless despair.

The above is fresh—just happened to-day. Not new,
—they often do this.

ANOTHER, FROM THE SAME.

It is said of Joe Jefferson that he went into a bank in
St. Louis one day to get a check cashed, and when the
teller said, "You must be identified, I do not know you,"
the great impersonator of "Rip" turned towards the door
and said, sadly: "If my leedle dog Schneider vas heere
he vood know me." The teller called him back and
handed out the money, with the remark that no one but
Joe Jefferson could say it like that.

But the First National Bank of Red Oak, Iowa, had a
case of "dorg" last summer that was equal to the above.
They received by mail a postal-card, which read as follows:

BANKING HOUSE OF BROOKS & MOORE,
Reinbeck, Iowa, *March* 6, 1878.
CASHIER 1ST NAT. BK.,

Dear Sir:—Mr. A. Moyer goes from here to your
part of the State by wagon, and carries our drafts, Nos.

1659 for $708.00.
1660 for $709.00 $1417.00

which please cash for him if desired. Mr. M. is a short,
middle-aged man, and will be accompanied by a yellow
bull-dog.   Respectfully,

L. T. MOORE, *Cashier.*

In due time a little stub and twist man stepped into the door of the 1st National at Red Oak, and then, as if he had suddenly thought of something left outside, stepped out again, and shouted, "Here! Come here!" When he reappeared he was accompanied by the unmistakable bull-dog, "with his ears cut short and his tail cut long," and built after the model of his master, and when he got his eye on the cashier, it is needless to say Mr. Moyer got his money.

CASHIER AND RUNNER.

One of the wits of Munster bar was Ned Lysaght, who startled a Dublin banker, one day, as he was walking home from the bank, by asking him for employment in the bank.

"*You*, my dear Lysaght!" exclaimed the banker, "what situation in my concern would suit you?"

"I could manage two if you'd let me."

"Tell me what they are," said the astonished banker.

"If you let me act as your *cashier* for one day, I'll turn *runner* the next," replied the wag.

A "COOKE" ITEM.

Not a thousand years ago, at a party given by one of our great bankers, who had made his millions on government securities—five-twenties and the like—a lady wit pointed out to her companion, also a banker, the wife of the host, remarking, "What a splendid creature ! She ought to be a *Countess !*"   "Oh, yes ; beautiful enough and clever enough ; but perhaps she prefers to be a *Discountess !*"

AN IRISH BULL.

"If I place my money in the savings bank," inquired a newly-arrived, "when can I draw it out again ?"

"Oh," responded his Hibernian friend, " sure, an' if you put it in to-day, you can get it out again to-morrow, by giving a fortnight's notice."

INTERESTING LAW.

The following is a literal copy of an Act of the Hawkeye State Legislature of 1858 :

"The first day of the week, commonly called Sunday, the first day of January, the fourth day of July, the twenty-fifth of December, and any day appointed or recommended by the Governor of this State, or the President of the United States, as a day of fast or thanksgiving, shall, for all purposes whatsoever, as regards the presenting for payment or acceptance, and of the protesting and giving notice of the dishonor of bills of exchange, bank checks and promissory notes, be treated and considered *as falling due on the succeeding day.*"

OVERMUCH PRECAUTION.

A wealthy banker, preparing to visit the Paris Exposition by ocean steamer, prudently purchased a costly safe to put in his state-room, for protection of his valuables in case the vessel was destroyed by fire.

———•———

A second-hand bookseller once posted the following announcement :

" For sale here—
Mill on Political Economy.
do. on the Floss."

———•———

A FINANCIAL PUZZLE.

This, now, is straightforward and business-like : A. applied to B. for a loan of $100. B. replied, " My dear A., nothing would please me more than to oblige you, and I'll do it. I haven't $100 by me, but make a note and I'll indorse it, and you can get the money from the bank." A. proceeded to write the note. " Stay," said B., "make it $200. I want $100 myself." A. did so, B. indorsed the paper, the bank discounted it, and the money was divided. When the note became due, B. was in California, and A. had to meet the payment. What he is unable to cipher out is whether he borrowed $100 of B., or B. borrowed $100 of him.

JUDICIAL RESOLUTIONS.

During the discussion of a bill for the funding of a certain State debt, a luminous member from the rural districts tied up all debate in the Legislature by submitting this mixture:

Resolved, That it is imperative that the old bonds of indebtedness be taken up.

Resolved, That in order to take up the aforesaid old bonds, new bonds be issued.

Resolved, That the new bonds do not be issued until the old bonds are surrendered.

A New York paper, speaking of a Russian loan of thirty thousand roubles, very quietly said by its types, that "the Russian government had advertised for a loan of thirty thousand *troubles*."

HAD TO PAY "ALLE SAME."

A friend at Los Angeles, California, sends us an account of a lawsuit in the local court of that place, brought by a Chinaman to recover $125. The note on which the suit was brought was of itself a wonder. It was written in Chinese characters, and fills five columns, reading from right to left. The translation is as follows, the reader bearing in mind that in China "he" stands for both sexes:

This woman, Sim Yip, he wantee catchee one hundred twenty-five dollars, gold coin. He say, sposum Yo Hing let um hap one hundred twenty-five dollars, gold coin, Sim Yip he pay um back in six months, with two per cent. interest. Fung Chong, he say, sposum Sim Yip no pay him money, he, Fung Chong, payee him alle same.

As Mrs. Yip failed to pay, Yo Hing sued Fung Chong, a Chinese doctor, on this guarantee, and when the plaintiff's counsel asked him about the note, he answered:

"Yo Hing one big rascal. He foolee you big heap muchee. Me showee in court how he foolee you."

But he did not, and to his infinite disgust the court gave judgment against him. Mr. Hing got his cash "allee same."

BURNING A BANKER'S NOTES.

During one of the rebellions in Ireland, the rebels, who had conceived a high degree of indignation against a certain great banker, passed a resolution that they would at once burn his notes, which they held; this they accordingly did, forgetting that, in burning his notes, they were destroying his debts, and that for every note which went into the flames, a corresponding value went into the banker's pocket and out of their own. This is what may be termed a genuine financial Hibernianism!

BANKS FAILING.

" Are you afraid of the banks failing ?" asked a Boston cashier, as Mrs. Partington went to draw her pension. "Banks failing !" said the dame ; " I never had any idea about it at all.   If he gets votes enough I don't see how he can fail, and if he don't, I can't see how he is to help it."   "I mean," said he, "the banks that furnish paper for the currency."   She stood a moment counting her bills.   "Oh, you did, did you ?" said she ; " well, it's about the same thing.   If they have money enough to redeem with—and heaven knows there's need enough for 're-demption' for a good many of them, and more 'grace' than they allow their customers—they may stand it ; but doubtful things are uncertain."

She passed off like an exhalation, and the cashier counted out $115.17 fifteen times while pondering what she said, in order to catch her meaning.

LARGE BONDS.

The young gentleman who officiates as countist in one of the Ithaca banks, mentions a little incident that occurred there in 1864, when the farmers were investing liberally in seven-thirty notes.

One day a lank countryman entered the bank, and leaning over the counter until his face almost touched mine, said, in a drawling tone : " Have you got any of

them *seven by nine bonds?* If you have, I want some."
Taking out his "pus" and counting the required sum,
he obtained his governments and evaded the premises.

THE WIDOW'S PROTEST.

One of the saddest things that ever came under my
notice (said the banker's clerk) was there in Corning,
during the war. Dan Murphy enlisted as a private, and
fought very bravely. The boys all liked him, and when
a wound by and by weakened him down, till carrying a
musket was too heavy work for him, they clubbed together and fixed him up as a sutler. He made money
then, and sent it always to his wife to bank for him. She
was a washer and ironer, and knew enough by hard experience to keep money when she got it. She didn't
waste a penny. On the contrary, she began to get mi-
serly as her bank account grew. She grieved to part
with a cent, poor creature, for twice in her hard-working
life she had known what it was to be hungry, cold, friendless, sick, and without a dollar in the world, and she had
a haunting dread of suffering so again. Well, at last
Dan died; and the boys, in testimony of their esteem
and respect for him, telegraphed to Mrs. Murphy to
know if she would like to have him embalmed and sent
home; when you know the usual custom was to dump a
poor devil like him into a shallow hole, and *then* inform
his friends what had become of him. Mrs. Murphy

5

jumped to the conclusion that it would only cost two or
three dollars to embalm her dead husband, and so she
telegraphed " Yes." It was at the "wake" that the bill
for embalming arrived and was presented to the widow.

She uttered a wild, sad wail that pierced every heart,
and said, " Sivinty-foive dollars for stooffin' Dan, blister
their sowls ! Did thim divils suppose I was goin' to
stairt a Museim, that I'd be dalin' in such expinsive
curiassities ?"

The banker's clerk said there was not a dry eye in the
house.

—*Mark Twain's Sketches.*

DISGUSTED WITH BANKS.

Since the failure of the late Freedman's Savings
Bank, our bank has been the agent of many depositors
in that concern for the collection of their dividends from
Washington. The charge for collecting is fifteen cents or
more, according to amount due the customer. The first
dividend of twenty per cent. had been nearly all paid,
when there came to our window one day the anxious face
of a man who had just heard " dey was issuin' out on
de ole firm," and who eagerly presented his pass-book.

We explained the terms of collection as above, to
which he agreed ; but on examination of his book he
appeared to have but fifty cents due him, and so we advised him not to put in his claim, as the amount received
would be less than the cost of getting it. " An' is I got

to lose my hard-earned money, boss?" he said, pathetically. "No, we can collect it for you for fifteen cents ; but you'll only get ten cents at this payment, and so you'll be five cents out. Hadn't you better let it be as it is?" This puzzled him. "I pays you fifteen cents, an' gits only ten? Whah's *my* money comin' from den?" The case was a hopeless one, and we could only advise him to call in person at the Washington office of the commissioners, as the sole way to receive his money without expense. He departed muttering, " Dat's why I 'spise a bank! I'll never put any mo' money into no bank, if all de bank men starves 'emselves to deff!" From the general tightness of the market, it is presumed he is sticking to his resolution.

FINAL ARGUMENT AT A BANK COUNTER.

On receipt of the news of the banks suspending specie payment, Mrs. Jones hastened to her savings bank, elbowed her way smartly to the desk, presented her book, and demanded her money.

" Madam," said the clerk, persuasively, "are you sure you want to draw this money out in specie?"

"Mrs. Jones," said a director, with an oracular frown, "do you know that you are injuring your fellow-depositors?"

"And setting an example of great folly to less-educated persons in this community?" struck in another director.

"Let us advise you simply to reflect," interposed the clerk, blandly.

"To wait for a day or two, at least," said the director.

At last there was a pause.

Mrs. Jones had been collecting herself. She burst now. In a tone which was heard throughout the building, and above all the din, and at which her interlocutors turned ashy pale, she said:

"*Will you pay me my money—yes or no?*"

They paid her instantly.

———◆———

BALL-ROOM TIME-TABLE.

A witty lady, writing of the grand ball once given in Philadelphia by Mr. Jay Cooke, the great banker and Government-bond broker, says: "The company commenced to arrive at 5.20; dancing began at 7.30; supper was served at 10.40!"

———◆———

GERMAN FINANCIAL OPERATION.

There were once two well-known settlers in the western part of York County, Pa., both of honest old German stock, and belonging to those good old times when everybody was "as honest as the days are long." Peter, it appears, had increased the size of his farm by annexing thereto a small tract adjoining, and lacked about one hundred dollars of the sum necessary to pay for the new acquisition. He called upon his neighbor, George, to borrow the amount.

George brought out an old bread-basket, and counted down the desired number of "thalers," and then, of course, the two sat down to two large earthen mugs of cider, and so many pipes of tobacco.

After smoking over the matter for a while, it occurred to Peter that in similar transactions he had heard or seen something like a "note" passing between the borrower and the lender, and he suggested as much to George.

The lender assented to the reasonableness of the thing ; paper, pen and ink were produced—and between the two a document was concocted, stating that George had loaned Peter one hundred dollars, which Peter would repay to George in "dree monts."

This Peter signed, and thus far our two financiers had made the thing all regular and ship-shape.

But at this point a difficulty presented itself. They both knew that notes were made in the operations of borrowing and lending, which they had sometimes witnessed ; but it now appeared that neither had observed what disposition was made of the document, nor could tell whether it was *en regle* for the borrower or lender to take charge of the paper,—and here was a dilemma ! At length a bright idea struck George.

"You has de money to pay, Peter ; so be sure you must take dis paper so you can see as you has to pay it."

This was conclusive ; the common sense of the thing was obvious and unanswerable, and Peter pocketed the money and his note, "so as he would see as he had to pay it."

The three months passed over, and punctually to the day appeared our friend Peter, and paid over the promised sum to George. This being done, the mugs and pipes were again paraded. After puffing awhile, Peter produced the note, and handed it to George, with the remark ;

"Now you must take de note, so as you can see dat de money has been paid."

FEMALE FINANCIERING.

One of our wealthy customers having occasion to leave town for a few days, left a dozen checks signed in blank for use of his better half, who proceeded, of course, to overdraw his account. On his return he remonstrated, but to no purpose ; for the fair but unsophisticated Dulcinea insisted that it couldn't possibly be, as there were three of the checks left now' which hadn't been used at all ! John is discouraged.

A TELLER WHO KNEW HIS BUSINESS.

An incident occurred the other day in an institution not a thousand miles from Lindsay, Ontario, which is thus related by the *Post* of that town. The inspector from the parent bank was paying his usual visit, and had among other things counted the teller's cash, which was found "O. K." On returning the cash to the teller, the latter at once carefully counted it. The inspector, a little surprised, asked the cause of this needless ceremony, whereupon the teller replied that he "never allowed any man to handle his cash without counting it after him." The result of this cool reply and business method was a prompt and handsome increase in the teller's salary.

------◆------

WHICH MAIDEN NAME?

The regulations of this savings bank require, that depositors furnish certain items of information concerning themselves, to be recorded for the purpose of identifying the depositors, when occasion requires; among which items is required the *mother's maiden name* of the depositor.

One young woman, on opening a deposit account, and being asked what was her mother's maiden name, said, " Which one ? for she had been married twice."

" *Mariners' Savings Bank, New London, Ct.*"

------◆------

PAR.

One often hears quoted certain expressions illustrative of "the ruling passion strong in death ;" but we have heard of none better than that of a venerable woman, the grandmother of a banker, who had reached the age of ninety-nine years and eight months.

Feeling very weak one morning she sent for the doctor, and in the course of the interview, asked him if he thought she would attain the age of one hundred.

"Well, Madam, you may depend upon my doing my best," he replied. "Oh, do !" said the old lady, "I should *so much* like to touch '*par.*'"

SCOTCH SIMPLICITY.

Here's an amusing incident of Scotch simplicity. An old "wifie," having heard whispers that the Caledonian was shaky, thought she would be on the safe side, went to the bank and presented her check for the balance. The cashier checked it in Caledonian bank-notes, which the canny old lady pocketed, and walking across to the National Bank asked them to exchange these for their own notes, which, having obtained, she went bank again to her own bank, and handing them over to the teller, said :—"There, that's the 'richt' paper. Will ye just take care of them for me?" Two days after the Caledonian suspended payment.

HOW THEY FIXED IT.

A New Yorker, while journeying the other day, was recognized by another citizen doing business near the

Bowery, he being also away from home on business, and after a little preliminary conversation the first remarked :

"Well, I hear that you had to make an assignment."

"Yes, dat is drew," replied the other.

"And your brother over on Chatham street; he assigned, too, didn't he?"

"You zee it was just like dis," said the Bowery man; "I was owing a goot deal. I makes over my stock to Jacob and Jacob makes over his stock over to me, and I do his peesness and he does my peesness, and dem vellers vhat was after money doan get some!"

THE GRASSHOPPER AND THE ANT.

A frivolous Grasshopper, having spent the summer in Mirth and Revelry, went on the Approach of the inclement Winter to the Ant, and implored it of its charity to stake him. "You had better go to your Uncle," replied the prudent Ant; "had you imitated my Forethought and deposited your Funds in a Savings Bank, you would not now be compelled to regard your Duster in the light of an Ulster." Thus saying, the virtuous Ant retired, and read in the Paper next morning that the Savings Bank where he had deposited his Funds had suspended.

Moral.—Dum Vivimus Vivamus.

—*" Out of the World" Fables.*

5*

DOCTOR G. JONES.

The writer was once employed as cashier by a gentleman whom we will call George Jones, whose knowledge
of book-keeping was extremely limited. The cashier's
custom was to keep his payments and receipts of cash on
slips of paper, which were stuck on a spindle until the
close of business, when they were transferred to the
cash-book. One day the proprietor came in and asked
for fifty dollars for personal use, which was handed him,
the cashier making out a slip, viz.: Dr. Geo. Jones, $50,
and impaling it on the spindle. On turning to resume
his work on the books he was very much surprised and
considerably amused on hearing his employer inquire, in

a severe tone: "Mr. D——, what do you mean, sir, by writing me down as *Doctor* George Jones?"

It is needless to say that a satisfactory explanation was made on the spot.

———◆———

VERY HOPEFUL INVESTMENT.

The wit who put this leaf into Harper's "Drawer" deserves a pension, and a good long life to enjoy it:

"Can you give me specie for this?"

"No!"

"What can you give me?"

"Nothing."

"Nothing? Why?"

"You are making a 'run' upon our institution—*a run*, sir. This species of presentation we are bound to resist. You are trying to break us, sir—to make us stop payment, sir. But you can't *do it*, sir."

"But *haven't* you stopped payment when you refuse to redeem?"

"No, sir. Ours is a *stock* institution. Your ultimate security, sir, is deposited with the auditor. We *can't* break, sir—we *can't* stop payment."

"But have you no specie on hand?"

"Yes, sir; and we are bound to KEEP it on hand; the law *obliges* us to keep twelve and one-half of specie on hand. If we paid it out every time one of you fellows calls, how, sir, could we 'keep it on hand,' according to law? We should be in a *pretty* box."

"Then I shall proceed to have the note protested."

"Very well, sir, you will find a notary public at ——, provided he is at home. He lives about one hundred and forty miles from here. But you'd better go home, sir, and rely upon your ultimate security. We *can't* pay specie, find it won't do—but you are ultimately secure."

The "ultimate security" is disregarded, the note is protested, "without regard to *expense*," and the notary directed to prosecute the "Squash Bank at Lost Prairie," to collection, as soon as possible. "How long, by the way," asks the holder, "will it be before I can expect to realize upon the ultimate security of the institution? Thirty days, is it not?"

"Not quite so soon as *that*, sir. I shall forthwith give notice to the officers of the Squash Bank. If they pay no attention to it, I shall offer its securities in my hands for sale; but in discharging my necessary duty to *all* the creditors of the institution, I shall not proceed to offer any of its assets in this market until after at least ninety days' notice in New York, London and Paris, so as to insure the largest and best prices for the securities—and not even then, if, in my opinion, the ultimate interests of all concerned will be promoted by a further extension! Hem!"

"But, my dear sir, how long will it be before I shall be able to actually realize upon my demand?"

To this pregnant question the notary replies that "he couldn't say, indeed; it depends something on the fate of the war in Europe—even now more doubtful than ever. Still, you can rely upon your ultimate security."

"ULTIMATE SECURITY—but I—I want *my money !*"

"Oh, ay, ah ! that's a different thing !"

This was what might be termed a very "hopeful" investment.

———————

HOOSIER ENGLISH.

A few years ago, two very respectable gentlemen commenced business as bankers, in one of the thriving villages of Illinois. It is quite common for business-men to have a little card printed on one corner of their envelopes, and these bankers, conforming to usage, printed theirs, giving their name and residence, and underneath, in smaller type, the following extraordinary announcement :

"Collections promptly attended to, and remitted *on day of judgment.*"

It took them several months to learn why their collecting business did not prosper.

———————

BANKS OF EASE.

About the beginning of the present century, the old Bank of Albany, since defunct, then presided over by thirteen distinguished representatives of Father-land, issued its first circulating notes. Immediately after their receipt from the printer, an application for a loan of a few thousand dollars was made to the bank by a drawee, well known in Albany for his ability and financial soundness.

The loan was "passed" by the board, and the cashier ordered to pay the money, who, like a faithful officer, bethought himself as to what *kind* of money he would pay—whether their own new currency or gold. The currency was new; so he reconvened the directors at once, and laid the subject before them.

Chairs were drawn to the great fire-place, thirteen clay pipes were lighted, and discussion ensued upon the proposition to pay out the new currency. No satisfactory conclusion was likely to be arrived at, until the following speech was made by one of the number :

"Gentlemen of the board, these bills of ours, received to-day, have cost this bank a large sum of money. The engraver, the printer, the paper-maker, and incidentals, all have to be paid. The thought of these expenses, so justly incurred, does not stagger me in the least, for the bills are very fine, and an ornament to the bank. But, gentlemen, when it is proposed to send these new bills into the far West, there to be traded for cattle, torn, soiled, and perhaps utterly destroyed, I, for one, most solemnly protest. I venture this moment, gentlemen, to assert the opinion, that should you be so unwise as to allow these new bills to be sent North and West, beyond Lansingburg, Schenectady, and away the other side of Utica (as I understand this man proposes to take some of them), you will never see them again so long as the Bank of Albany has an existence or a name !"

The motion was lost, and the gold was duly paid. Surely this bank might well be termed a Bank of Ease.

"OLD VINTER'S" BANK BILLS.

Away Down East—that convenient but much abused locality for pointing a story—a wealthy old merchant, who was especially fond of a glass of good brandy, had established a bank, and, liking his own face better than any one's else, showed his frankness by placing it on both ends of his bank bills. One evening a bill of this description was offered at the village hotel, and was thought to be a counterfeit. "Put a glass of brandy to the picture," proposed a wag, "and if his mouth opens, you may be sure it is one of old Vinter's."

BUSINESS AND BEAUTY.

The deficiency in the practical part of female education is a fact which has been often, but never too much, deplored. The following notes of an examination instituted by a mercantile gentleman in search of a wife, into a young lady's knowledge of business, is testimony complete on this point.

Young lady, examined: Has heard of the monetary question; should think it was a warning. Knew what stocks were; regards them as the "highest necessity" in a gentleman's dress. A dividend was a sum in long division. A bonus was a sort of a pill. Scrip was a little bag—something like a reticule. Exchange was no robbery. Had read about consols—they were ancient

Romans; Julius Cæsar was one, so was Pompey. Supposed by three per cents must mean the Triumvirate. A bull was a horned animal, or an Irish mistake. A bear was a cross, disagreeable person, like some people she could name. An exchequer bill was an instrument with a hook. The bullionists were a religious sect. Was afraid the inconvertibles were very wicked people. Gold was a metal; knew nothing more about it, except that it was the root of all evil, and that railway cuttings and branch banks come of the root

———•———

BLUFF IDENTIFICATION.

The late E. M. S., of Cincinnati, was a rough diamond of the first water, who had little patience with *airy* people. Going into M——'s bank one day, he presented a check payable to his own order, which M. in person threw back, saying pompously, "Don't know you, sir!" S. stepped back, and gazing at the banker from head to feet, rejoined, "That's just my fix exactly, sir! I've been in this town, man and boy, for twenty-seven years, and *I never heard of you before!*"

The money was paid over to him without another word.

———•———

INDORSER'S QUALIFICATIONS.

A worthy but poor minister once requested the loan of fifty dollars from the cashier of a country bank; and in the note requesting the favor, he said that if the cashier would oblige him, he would "pay him in ten days, on the faith of Abraham." The cashier returned word that, by the rules of the bank, the indorser of the note must reside in the State !

DISCOUNTING A HIBERNIAN'S NOTE.

A transparent Hibernian wanted a friend to discount a note. "If I advance this," said the lender, "will you pay your note punctually ?" "I will, on my honor," replied the other—"*the expense of the protest and all !*"

PANIC BLUNDERS—WRONG CERTIFICATE AT THE BANK.

In the midst of one of the worst of our business panics, and at the moment when everybody thought all the banks were going to the dogs together, Jones—the inevitable Jones—rushed into the bank of which he was a stockholder, and thrusting the certificate into the face of the transfer clerk, he said in great haste, " Here, please transfer half that to James P. Smith !" The clerk looked at it and asked, " Which half, Mr. Jones ?" " I don't care which half," replied Jones, puzzled at the inquiry.

"You had better go to the courts ; I can't make the

transfer without a legal decision. If you really wish to transfer your other half to Mr. Smith, we can't do it here." Jones was confounded. He knew the banks were all in a muddle, but this was too deep for him. He took his certificate from the hand of the smiling clerk, and, on looking at it, lo! it was his *marriage* certificate! Being a printed form, on fine paper, and put away among his private papers, it was the first thing that Mr. Jones laid hands on when he went to his secretary for his bank-stock scrip. He went home, kissed his wife—glad to find she hadn't been transferred to Mr. Smith—and, taking the right papers this time, hastened down town, in season to get the matter all straight.

DUTCHMAN'S GOLD IN A SAFE PLACE AT LAST.

Everybody will remember the startling money panic they had at San Francisco some years ago, and the story John Phœnix used to tell of its effects—individually illustrated. Before the fright, an old Dutchman, by dint of hard labor, had accumulated some five hundred dollars, which he cautiously deposited in one of the banking-houses for safe-keeping. Rumors soon came to his ears that they were not very safe—some said that they had "broke." Next morning he tremblingly drew his balance, and put the shining gold into his pocket. He breathed decidedly freer, but here was a dilemma. What should he do with it? He did not dare to keep it in his shanty—and as for carrying it about with him, 'twas too precious heavy. So, after a sleepless night or two, in constant apprehension of burglars, he deposited it in another "banking-office." Another day—the panic increased—there was a run on his bank; he pushed in —drew his gold—and felt easier once more. Another anxious day and night for his "*monish*," and again it was deposited in a *safe* bank. This time he felt safer than ever before, and went quietly to his work. But the panic reached *that* bank, and anxious depositors besieged the doors. Mynheer heard the news, and put post haste, book in hand, for the scene of action—jammed in with the crowd—drew his gold, new and bright—put it safe in his corduroys—and was happy once more; but here was the dilemma fresh again—where to put it! He had gone pretty much the rounds of the banks, and having had such narrow escapes, couldn't and wouldn't trust them any more. He sat down on a curbstone and soliloquized thus: "I put mine monish in von bank, ven he preak; I put him in de oder bank, ven he preak too; I draw him out; I can no keep him home; I put him into dis bank, now dis one preak; vat te tuyvil shall I do? I *now* take him home and sew him up in my frou's petticoat, and if she preakes, I preakes—her head!"

———•———

Jimmy B., a frugal son of Erin, would once in a while have a wrestle with John Barleycorn. After one of these bouts he came to the bank in great excitement to notify the teller that his bank-book had been stolen, and added, vehemently, "If the *incindiary* comes, you must detict him !"

———————

H., the notary, "rotund, rubicund and jocund," was stepping into his buggy with a handful of unpaid notes, to go his rounds of presentation and demand. "Going out to *take the air?*" hailed an acquaintance. "Next thing to it," said H. ; "I'm going out to *raise the wind.*"

———————

Gottlieb Schneider sometimes wanted to collect by draft the account of a country customer. On such occasions he would get the collection clerk of the —— bank to fill up a draft for him. One day he dumb-foundered a new clerk by announcing to him, "I vants to *pull* on Maysville." It took some minutes to get up a mutual understanding, and to teach Gottlieb that pulling and drawing are not always the same.

———————

THE DISAPPOINTED BANKER.

Could anything be wittier for a banker than the following new and neat reply of Baron Rothschild, told by Arsène Houssaye? One of his friends, of the third degree, a sort of banker, came to borrow $2,000.

"Here it is," said the baron, "but remember that as a rule I only lend to crowned heads." M. de Rothschild never dreamed of seeing his money again, but, wonderful to relate, at the end of a month, the borrower came back with his $2,000. The baron could scarcely believe his eyes ; but he foreboded that this was not the end. Sure enough, a month later the borrower reappeared, asking for the loan of $4,000. "No, no," said the baron, "you disappointed me once by paying me that money. I do not want to be disappointed again."

A MINOR DISTINCTION.

The following is contributed by a Trojan :

The other day an intelligent-looking English woman came into our savings bank, wishing to deposit some money to the credit of George ———, the same name as that of her husband, who already had an account open. Supposing it to be her son, I said,

"Is he a minor ?"

"No," replied the lady ; "he's a blacksmith."

THE CASHIER'S DELIGHT.

[TIME LOCKS DISPENSED WITH.]

The *New York Graphic* recently contained the following unique sketch, illustrating the latest approved method of keeping the combination of the vault. The machine works admirably,—wherever it has been tried.

The inventor will now win the everlasting gratitude of all the banks, if he will so perfect his invention as to fit up a few thousand for the customer who talks, for the office bore, the peripatetic book agent, *et al.*

(From the *New York Daily Graphic*, October 29, 1878.)

PATENT COMPOUND DUPLEX ELLIPTIC LOCK FOR THE MOUTH OF THE BANK OFFICIAL WHO KNOWS THE "COMBINATION."

A NEW YORK DEAL.

Smith, Brown, Jones and Robinson own a mine. The property is incorporated—100,000 shares of the par value of $100 each. The stock is listed on the New York Mining Board, and Smith is in New York making a "deal." The office of the company is in this city, and the Secretary resides here, but he went fishing a few weeks since, and a friend of his was kind enough to consent to act as Secretary for him in his absence. One day Brown, who is one of the Directors of the Big Thing G. and S. M. Company, went into the office of the company, and the acting Secretary said to him :

"See here, Brown, you might give a fellow a show to make something in the Big Thing."

"Fact is," returned Brown, "there's not much doing in the stock here in San Francisco, but we hope to place it in New York, and that is why Smith is on there now. But being as it's you, I'll leave you have a thousand for four bits a share. There's not a share of the stock out, but Smith is watching it in New York, and we hope to create an interest in it and get people to buy it."

The acting Secretary took the stock and mailed it to a sharp mining broker friend in New York with instructions to sell it in the Mining Board. The friend received the stock and went into the board to sell it. When Big Thing was called, Smith's broker began to bid frantically for any number of shares at $2, and another one of Smith's brokers occasionally let him

have a ten or twenty share lot.　Pretty soon Broker No.
1 got desperate and bid $2.25 for 1,000.

"Sold," yelled the acting Secretary's friend.

And Smith, Brown, Jones and Robinson were sold,
and the acting Secretary got the money.

By return mail Brown heard the news, and, happen-
ing to drop into the office, he remarked to the acting
Secretary :　"There's something mysterious going on in
this here company.　There ain't a share of the stock out,
and Brown writes me from New York that he had taken
in a thousand at two and a quarter.　Where do you suppose it could have come from ?"

"I don't know to a certainty," replied the acting
Secretary, "but I got advices from my broker in New
York this morning that he had sold my thousand Big
Thing at two and a quarter, and putting this and that
together, you know————"

Brown did not wait to hear any more, but rushed
around to the telegraph office, and telegraphed to the
Secretary to come home and take charge of things d—n
quick, as everything in the office was going to rack and
ruin, and the man he had put on as a sub was a fraud
of the deepest dye.—*San Francisco Stock Report.*

AN UNSATISFACTORY ANSWER.

Mr. O'C——, a cotton merchant, and mayor of our
city of 10,000 people, drinks,—sometimes excessively.

Having occasion recently to present a draft of one of

FINANCERING IN THE OLDEN TIME.

A Directors' Meeting—A La Darwin.

his customers to him, which had been given to me by the —— Bank for protest, I found him considerably under the influence of John Barleycorn, as our conversation illustrates :

" Mr. O'C——, will you pay this draft ?"

" I reckon ze draf's allright, zit down a lil' while— when ze bo'keep'r comes in, he give you a shock—hic."

" But I can't take a check. Must have the money. It is in my hands for protest."

" Ze devil you can't ! Who shends you here wiz such a message as 'at ?"

" The —— Bank, sir."

" Well—hic—you tell ze —— Bank *to protess*—hic— an' *be dam ! Tell 'em zat.*"

The answer was duly noted and extended by the notary, who hopes the reply was as funny to all concerned as to him.   P.

CHINESE TIME.

The Chinese have a curious but very remarkable method of keeping time. If a Chinaman borrows five dollars of you, and agrees to return it in three days you can't catch sight of him for three weeks. If you borrow five dollars of him and agree to return it in three weeks, he calls at the end of three days and demands his cash.

Grand write and left was the forger's last change as he waltzed out of sight.

A QUEER TOAST.

At a dinner at the Mansion House, London, three foreign consuls were present, whom the Lord Mayor wished to honor by drinking their healths. He accordingly directed the toastmaster to announce the healths of "the three present consuls." He, however, mistaking the words, gave out the following: "The Lord Mayor drinks the health of the three per cent. consols."

———•———

When our Uncle Samuel decides to issue another new dollar, we shall be on hand to suggest the owl as a bird entitled to consideration in the matter of portraits. The bird of wisdom has been shabbily treated.

———•———

When you ask a Turkish fellow for that half dollar he owes you, don't say "hand us over that fifty cents," but, "See here, effendi, fork over that yrmilykmedjid."

———•———

Norfolk kept quiet, got to bed at a seasonable hour, lived economically, and is now the headquarters of the peanut trade of America.

———•———

The banker leads a loan-sum life.

CORRESPONDENCE.

"Never write a letter—never destroy one."
—GOETHE'S MEPHISTOPHILES.

SPECIMEN

OF SEVERAL HUNDRED LETTERS RECEIVED BY THE COMPILER HEREOF.

NOTE.—Running a bank is not altogether fun.

———, PA., *Dec.*, 1878.

DEAR SIR:—I am in receipt of your "announcement" of the "Cashier's Scrap-Book," and I assure you of my best wishes for its success. It is only necessary to tell *the truth* to make it one of the most thrilling books of the times. The writer hereof has been through one grand robbery of $150,000 by his own book-keeper—one failure of over $100,000—one hunt for *two days* for a lost special of $2,500, subsequently found adhering to the side of the safe by the aid of unnecessary gum Arabic—another hunt of *three days* for a package of $5,000, in large bills, supposed to be lost, but wasn't ; the *agony* of all of which is known only to him who "knows how it is himself."

I inclose a few items, and, wishing you all sorts of good luck,

I am, yours truly,

———, *Cashier.*

ALMOST A RUN.

A PRINCE EDWARD'S ISLAND INCIDENT.

To a student of human nature, no better place could be found for his studies than behind a bank counter. I have been no exception to the rule, but at the present time can only call to mind one incident worthy of a place in your book. It is illustrative of how easily a run may be caused on a bank by ignorant persons mistaking what one says.

Some years ago the writer was teller and acting accountant in a bank agency in ————. In this bank, as in many others, it was the custom to have a box attached to the outside of the counter, in which were deposited all notes offered for discount, and which was opened from time to time. While the teller was paying a large number of fishermen who had checks on the bank, the hour of twelve struck, after which time no notes would be received for discount. He asked the messenger who was standing outside the counter to see if there were any more *notes* in the box, and received as answer, "None, sir." To his astonishment, those fishermen who had not yet been paid turned and left the bank in a body, and rushed down the street and, as was afterwards found out, told every one they met that the bank had no more money. They went down to the office of the drawer of the checks, who returned with them, and matters were soon explained, but some people actually called at the bank to inquire if it was not in difficulties.

Yours truly,

—— ——.

——•——

SCRIPTURE CIPHER.

The cashier of the First National Bank of St. Paul, Minnesota, had occasion, some time ago, to notify the cashier of a bank in the southern part of the State that his account was overdrawn.   For answer he received the following telegram :

BANK OF ———, *June* 13, 1871.

Cashier First National Bank, St. Paul :

See Matthew, xviii. chapter, 29th verse.

Yours, —— ——, *Cashier.*

To which the following was promptly telegraphed back in reply:

FIRST NATIONAL BANK, ST. PAUL, *June* 13, 1871.

Cashier ——— Bank :

Examine Matthew, v. 25.

Yours, —— ——, *Cashier.*

The reader may search the Scriptures and find out the point.

——•——

SATISFACTORY IDENTIFICATION.

A number of years ago, when teller of this bank, a man presented a check payable to his order.   I wished him to be identified, and he said it was impossible, as he had no acquaintances in the city; and seemed quite disappointed. Suddenly a happy thought presented itself to him, and he began to unbutton his vest and pull up his shirt, remarking that it was all right, he had got his name on his shirt flap. It was such a novel idea, and the check being for a small amount, I concluded to pay, and he went away happy.   Yours,

FOSTER, *Cashier.*

SARCASTIC.

In September, 1871, a gentleman came into this bank and presented a check of one of our dealers, payable to Baldwin & Co., and asked for a draft on Chicago for the proceeds, which was given him; the draft being made payable to the order of Baldwin & Co. In a few days the draft was returned to the bank by S—— & C——, Bankers, ————, Wisconsin, without indorsement, with a request that we issue a new draft to their order in the place of it, or else send the money to their credit in Chicago, as the draft had not been made payable to the right person.

To this, reply was made as follows:

"THE STATE NATIONAL BANK OF KEOKUK,
" KEOKUK, IOWA, *September* 22, 1871.
"MESSRS. S—— & C——,
————, Wisconsin.

"Dear Sirs :—Your favor of 20th inst. is received, with an inclosure, $1,242.25. We cannot pay without

Baldwin & Co.'s indorsement, as we were directed to make it to their order. We have sent it to the bank at Pella, Iowa, to get the proper indorsement, and will report to you.   Very respectfully,

"—— ——, *Cashier.*"

By due course of mail this note was returned, with the following remark in pencil at the bottom of the sheet :

" Who in H—l asked you to make a draft payable to Baldwin & Co. ?

"S—— & C——."

To this the cashier replied, on the back of the same sheet, as follows :

" MESSRS. S—— & C——,

"Gentlemen :—Your inquiry on the opposite page hardly demands a courteous reply, but as it was doubt- less written while laboring under an attack of irritation, and we always intend to treat people with civility, I will say that the draft was drawn as asked for by Mr. Barron, as our teller understood it, and if not, Mr. B. was pres- ent, and had eyes to see if it was right. If you are bankers, you ought to know that we could not safely pay the draft or issue a new one without the indorse- ment of the payee. We did the next best thing—got it properly indorsed, and returned it to you a day or two since. The parties were all strangers to us.

"I will add that it was not in the place mentioned that he asked us to make the draft. We were never there, and do not expect to be, and we make this explanation, as we may never meet you.

"With due respect,

"—— ——, *Cashier*."

It is, perhaps, needless to add that there was no further correspondence.

———•———

LETTER FROM IOWA.

ANITA, IOWA, *February* 11, 1879.

Dear Sir :—Last summer, soon after Greenback clubs were formed here, the president of one of them was asked what he wanted to start a new party for, and what his principles were. Said he, "We haven't got our principles yet. We asked the man who came around starting the clubs, and he said *he hadn't any*, but they would be sent us from New York in a few weeks." Soon after resumption was proved a success, I asked him if he had his principles yet, and he said "Yes. I am for keeping the amount of greenbacks the same as at present, and always at par."

———

How will this do as a sample of thin security?

One day in midwinter, a stranger stepped into our office, and wanted a loan of $100, offering as security a chattel mortgage on his next crop of corn, and the following dialogue ensued :

"Where is your farm?"

"I don't own any land."

"What farm have you rented?"

"I haven't rented any yet, but I am going to rent one somewhere near this place."

The man was evidently in earnest, and seemed surprised because his "security" was considered "too thin."

Yours truly,

C. M. MYERS, *Cashier.*

A LADY BANK PRESIDENT.

[OFFICIAL ANNOUNCEMENT.]

STATE NATIONAL BANK OF RALEIGH,

RALEIGH, N. C., *Feb.* 10, 1879.

Dear Sir:—In a meeting of the board of directors of this bank, held to-day, Mrs. M. C. Williams and E. R. Stamps, Esq., were elected directors, and Mrs. M. C. Williams was elected president of the bank.

The signature of the president will be found below.

Respectfully, SAML. C. WHITE,

Cashier.

M. C. WILLIAMS,
President.

FROM A "FREEDMAN'S BANK CASHIER."

RICHMOND, Va., *Feb.* 12, 1879.

Some time during my cashiership in the Richmond office of the Freedman's Savings & Trust Co., a colored man presented a pass-book at the

6*

counter and desired to withdraw a sum of money. An examination showed the account to be in the name of his wife, who, under the act incorporating our bank, had exclusive control of her deposit, which could not be withdrawn without her presence, or a written order— this I informed the husband, and prepared a check for the amount, instructing the man to have his wife *make her mark* at the place designated, as she could not write, and have it witnessed by some person who could write. The man went out to obtain his wife's mark. After some time, he returned and handed me the check. I examined it, and found it in the same condition as when I gave it to him. A conversation somewhat similar to the following ensued.

Cashier.   I do not see any *mark* on the check.

Man.   She made her *mark.*

Cashier.   Where?

Man.   There—pointing to a torn corner of the check.

The woman had *torn off one corner of the check.* She had make *her mark* certain.   CHAS. SPENCER.

———•———

This is how a freedman made an "inquiration" as to his little deposit in the late Freedman's Savings & Trust Company :

                              *****, N ca Ap 27 174 AD.

Mr Purcer Cashir—

as I understand that the Freedman Bank, in Washington citty are about to be deprived of its pecuniary funds, and very likely to be broken you will pleas write

me whether or not.   You pleas give me true
financial information as you can concerning this Bank
and its discontented means, and I will be under many
obligations to you.   ·

Your most Honorable Friend,

——— ———.

———·———

LOUISVILLE EXPERIENCES.

Banking must be a delightful occupation in Louisville. The Scrap-Book has received the following letter,
which is its own explanation, and shows the wide range
of talent necessary for successful financiering in those
parts:

"OFFICE OF GERMAN SECURITY BANK,
"LOUISVILLE, KY., ———, 1879.

"I take it as a pleasure and privilege to furnish an
item for your book. Though a young banker of only
twelve years' experience, I have seen many funny things,
though perhaps hardly worthy of mention.

"Although an American, Kentuckian born, running
a bank originally gotten up by me, my influence among
the German population of our city, and as a German-
American Bank, has so united the two national influences as to make it (though I say it myself) the most
prosperous, as to dividends, of any bank in our city.
Since originating the bank, I have been looked upon, by
one portion of our population and my customers, as
having previously occupied myself with the legal fraternity ; by another, as having been previously a Methodist

or some other denominationalist preacher ; others again give me credit for having followed up the practice of medicine, and again, others think me a natural-born financier ; hence, I have had grave questions concerning all professions often propounded to me.

"One of the firm of S. & T., S., for instance, goes to Europe, leaving T. in charge. On return of S. he undertakes to examine the business and books in his absence ; finding T. (who is *Tobe*, and S., who is *Stockhoff*, both Germans) has lived on a remarkably small amount in his absence, demands to know how it is, and if he actually charged to himself (Tobe) the amount of cash he drew since his, S.'s, absence in Germany. Tobe says, 'Of course, I did not charge myself with all, for since I own one-half of the store, I would be a d—— fool to charge myself with ten dollars when I only draw ten ; but in such cases I always charged myself with five dollars ;' and in explanation said to S., 'Don't one-half the store belong to me ?' 'Yes.' 'Well, why then do I charge myself with what belonged to me ?' S. scratches his head, said that looked fair, but they would both call on Mr. B. (that's me), and he could soon settle it ; and notwithstanding my very plain explanation that T. should, during the absence of S., have charged himself with every dollar in full that he drew, without discount ; and that, on his principle, he might have sold the entire store out during S.'s absence, for cash, pocketed all the money, and only charged himself with one-half, and on S.'s return have divided the remaining half, thus giving him, T., three-quarters of the whole, and S. one-quarter of the whole, who, on going to Europe, was owner of one-half, T. was not satisfied, and I looked upon as a prejudiced arbitrator; and while he, T., had agreed to abide my arbitration, would do it; but one thing was d—— certain, he would at once dissolve with S., a man who would take advantage of such one-sided arbitration—and so the firm of S. & T. dissolved.

"Applications for legal documents, such as partnerships, deeds, mortgages, &c., are daily made under the impression I had been a lawyer, and such things could be done through me for *nothing*. The times I have been called to the death-bed of a former depositor, and asked to sing and pray, are numerous; and while I claim to sing very bass or base, I am not much on the pray; but I worry through with it, strange to say. Yet the study of both law and theology have always been the most foreign to my inclinations. I had a firm to deposit with me under firm name of D. Davis & Co. Wertheimer was the Company. Having the most money in the firm, W. desired his name to be more conspicuous in the firm, and notified me that hereafter his old firm would sail under the new firm name of W. & D. Davis. I undertook to explain that such sign would indicate that the firm was composed of W. Davis & D. Davis, but he could not see it, and so the firm name is to this day.

"Often in sickness have I been called upon by my German constituency, under the belief I was formerly an M. D., to prescribe. Being so successful, with the use of a few of Cook's Compound Cathartic Pills, which I happened to have in my pocket when called upon to visit the sick patient, I have ever since bought them for such occasions by the wholesale, and administer them to every patient who sends for me, regardless of the complaint, and have reason to congratulate myself that I have never been called on the second time by the same patient.   Of course, I cured them all.

"Financially, I am called on daily by my depositors, who have more money than is doing them good, to know how an investment in this, that, or the other will do. Fortunately, so far, I have been successful in my advice to ninety-nine out of a hundred; but one out of a hundred, acting on my advice, has missed it, and invariably comes back on me for redress, and insists that, inasmuch as they have made a loss on certain speculations under my advice, I should make up the loss; the ninety-nine out of every hundred who did well under similar advice never express any gratitude or opinion further than I had done nothing more than was my duty to do; all of which has almost forced me to the determination that I will place a placard in the office of the bank, 'The cashier was never a lawyer, a doctor, nor a minister, and is rapidly concluding that he is no financier, and those who insist to the contrary, and will be advised, must in future pay the usual fee;' and that 'Marrying, where the bride is pretty, and he is accorded the first kiss, will in future be made a specialty.'

"Yours truly,

"Cashier of bank named in caption."

BANKING IN COLORADO.

Dear " Scrap-Book :"—As story-telling seems to be in order, I wish to relate a little Missouri experience.

Early in 1871, the writer helped start a bank in southwest Missouri. Until better quarters could be obtained, we rented the office of the leading hotel of the place, that had formerly been used as a bar-room.

A few days after our occupation of the aforesaid room, a chap about six feet five in his stockings, and with a voice like the first rumblings of an earthquake, clad in the time-honored "homespun," stalked in, and after looking cautiously around, said : " *Set 'em eout, mister.*" Thinking the fellow was crazy, we blandly asked what we could do for him. With this he drew himself up to his full *perpendicular*—so to speak—and said : " *I know it air agin the law to sell licker to a chap as isent vouched for, but I am jest from Texas, and want about a mule's ear full of the strongest whisky you have in your shop, and no foolin' either.*" And we could hardly make the man believe that we were trying in our humble way to run a bank, and *not* selling whisky " on the sly." The last few years have made many changes, and the aforesaid bank, which has assumed the title of ———— National Bank, has to deal with a different class of humanity. No more does the youth from the extreme rural districts come in with the " *Heow much do you pay for coon skins ?*" or " *Mister, what do you keep here ?*" or, " How do you sell postage stamps ?" &c. Yours,

COLORADO.

AN INCIDENT OF THE PANIC.

WINONA, MINNESOTA.

An Irish woman held against us two or three certificates for amounts, in the aggregate some three hundred dollars. Some one the evening previous told her that the banks all over the country had *failed*, that none of them were good ; that alarmed her, and how to get her money on her certificates brought out her Irish wit ; so, before the bank opened the next morning, she made her appearance on the steps of the bank. Soon after I went in she followed me, and before saying a word began to cry vigorously. I asked her what was the matter, and between sobs she said, " *Oh, my poor child is most dead !*" I, of course, told her of my sympathy for her, and that probably her child would yet get well, &c., &c. But she kept repeating with her sobs—" my poor child—oh, my poor child will die !" While this was going on, she begun to feel around under the *top of her dress in front,* and drew out one of her certificates and handed me ; I told her all right, and handed her the money. Still crying for her *poor child*, she pulled out from the same place another, for which I also handed her the money ; she gave a *fresh cry*, and drew forth another and the last one. I also handed the money for this one. She departed, and the last I heard her say, was, " Oh, my poor child !"

The facts, when I inquired in regard to her, were, she had no *children*, sick or well, but adopted that plan before coming to the bank to work up sympathy, in order, as she supposed, to enable her to get her certificates cashed.

The banks in this city did not, for a single day, fail to meet every demand on them, and had ample resources for every emergency.

Yours very truly,

MARK WILLSON, *President.*

———◆———

"HOW EASY TO BE MISTAKEN."

While I was connected with Farmers' Bank of Kentucky at Mount Sterling, Kentucky, one of our best and most favored depositors came in, filled a check, and drew $100; in about two or three days he returned, and presenting a ten dollar counterfeit note, desired me to redeem it, feeling certain that I had paid it to him in the $100. I called his memory to the fact that I had paid him in twenties, and that I could never have passed such a glaring counterfeit. All I said was to no purpose; and as he swore that he had not changed, paid out, or handled the money since I paid him, he could not be mistaken; and growing more angry still, demanded his balance, and quit the office, as he said, forever. In a few days he again returned—this time, with a smile on his face, and brimful of apologies—saying that when he went home he was telling his better-half how shamefully I had treated him, when she told him that, wanting a twenty dollar bill to send off in a letter, she had gone to his purse, withdrawn a twenty and put two tens in its place. The old gentleman says he may be swindled by a cashier in the future, but he'll never believe it.

Wishing you success, and expecting many hearty laughs from "Our Scrap-Book,"

I am, very truly,

A. S. MITCHELL, *Cashier.*

FROM ONEIDA, NEW YORK.

H. C. PERCY, *Cashier,*

Dear Sir :—My attention has been called to a circular issued by you, requesting certain items growing out of bank transactions; and having been the Treasurer of a Savings Bank for twelve years, I am tempted to state one which, perhaps not entirely new, was nevertheless quite new as well as amusing to me.

A farmer living some half a dozen miles from our bank, and who not unfrequently made deposits with us, called one day and inquired if we had money to loan, and if we would loan it on a good note. He was told that we had money to loan, but did not loan it on notes alone. That to get money on a note of us it must have the additional security of suitable collaterals. He enquired what collaterals would answer? and was told that good stocks would be required. He came in a few days after, laid down his note, and said with a confident air that he would take three hundred dollars. I inquired as to his collaterals—what they were. He replied, horses and oxen and cows. He was told that the stocks referred to were government bonds, state bonds, &c. He said he had none of that particular kind of stock, and left quite disappointed.

Oneida Savings Bank.

———————◆———————

This corner was reserved for a poem from an Indiana Banker (Auburn), and this is what he sent.

Dear Sir :—I should like to send you a Wegglian Idyl or so, but having a child's obituary (one of our best customers' "cherished and only ") immediately, and a Decoration-Day poem soon to evolve, I must refrain. Let me add that I " know enough to know " that you have struck a rich vein, and I am sure it will be worthily worked.

I once sent out a draft for acceptance, and the acceptor wrote across it *Adopted.*

A party asked if we would loan money and take bonds as *calamity*—security. Another wanted to know if he did not pay his note when due, if we would *detest* it.

Another customer, in accepting paper, invariably writes in bold type, "Excepted :" but as he always pays, we take no exception thereto.   *

———————◆———————

One of Her Majesty's bank managers in Canada favors us with the following :

An Irishman, after an absence of eighteen years, returned to visit his relatives, with about sixteen hundred dollars in gold, the result of hard labor in the diggings during that time.

He obtained a deposit receipt for the gold, which had three months to run before it bore interest ; long before that the smiles of his friends had drawn all his spare cash, and often, under the influence of old rye, he had to make varied excuses for breaking his receipt, for which he was admonished with as much severity as was justifiable, by his banker.

Being a bachelor, he loved children, and has been seen with two of them, one in each hand, marching them along the main street, while they gallantly swayed huge sticks of candy, like barbers' poles, with their disengaged hands. These and similar aberrations from consistency brought him to his bed, where a doctor and the parish priest had to administer their respective consolations.

The following is his last appeal for another hundred ; the next appeal for the deposit receipt came from his nearest kin, through the probate court.

> "MOUNT ST. PATRICK
> "P. O. RINFREW COUNTY.

" Mr.

"Sir :—I happened to get sick here I think I will have to send for a doctor I have no money, It would be like getting it for nothing for me to get one hundred dollars from you now I want it bad and as you respect yourself as A Gentleman as I do you the same do send me the Above Amount for in the word of A Man I want it very bad.

"The Above is my Address MICHAEL MADIGAN.

"God Bless you.

"If you like you can send the money to the P. P. of this place.

"If you don't send me the money demanded I will be badly off."

"M. M."

———◆———

SPICY CORRESPONDENCE.

NATIONAL BANK ———,
IOWA, 1879.

A bookseller in Michigan shipped this bank a box of books, to be delivered to their agent in installments and remitted for. The agent refused to receive the books, and after considerable delay and correspondence, the box was shipped to the owner at his request, and he sent the bank twenty-five cents in three-cent postage stamps to pay the drayage (no other charge being made). The stamps were stuck on by the edge (as usual), and were nearly destroyed in tearing them off. The cashier in acknowledging the receipt of them, took occasion to say, in a civil and respectful manner, that a good way to send stamps by letter was to touch the tongue to the center of the stamps, and then they could be used as well as if new.

This elicited the following reply :

"———, MICH., *March* 3, 1879.

"My dear sir:—Your kind and very witty favor of February 28 to hand. We hope you will be able to use the stamps.   We are anxious to secure the services of a real wit, as correspondent.   Lacking both wit and beauty ourselves, we have decided that if you are as handsome as you are humorous, we will offer you the place.   Will you please send us your photo., or a clear and compendious description of yourself, or, what will be much more to the purpose, call on us, please, and so grant us the pleasure of a personal acquaintance.

"If you suit us, the amount of salary will not prevent our hiring you.   Please answer.

"Sincerely,   —— ——.''

The following reply was sent.

"—— NATIONAL BANK, *March*, 1879.

"Dear sir:—Your flattering letter of 3d inst. was duly received, and I felt very highly complimented by it. You are undoubtedly correct in your estimate of my humorous abilities, as they are freely admitted by all my acquaintances, although I do not often ' let myself out,' being occupied in the sterner duties of supporting a large family, and having but little leisure for the indulgence of my characteristic proclivities.

"I am not able to send you my picture, as I have never found an artist who was willing to risk his instruments upon me.   I shall, therefore, be obliged to content myself with a brief verbal description, viz.: Age, 29 past ; height, 6 feet 3¾ inches, in stockings ; weight, in ordinary working trim, 255 lbs.; complexion, dark ; eyes, black ; hair and beard, dark brown, full, and wavy; nose, slightly aquiline ; digestion good, and health robust.

"My disposition corresponds with my physique, and I am always good-natured and indulgent, and never suffer myself to be irritated or disturbed by any small thing. I am sorry that I am compelled to decline your generous offer, but I could not accept it without giving mortal offense to numerous friends and admirers who have tried to secure my services heretofore. I regret this the more, as it is very plain that you are an appreciative and discriminating gentleman, who can see wit and humor where no one else would discover it, and it is obvious from your contempt of small matters that you are a man of lofty and comprehensive views, and have not only the disposition, but the ability, to carry out your liberal ideas regardless of expense, as the patron and promoter of humble merit.

"Thanking you for your kindness, I remain,

"Yours sincerely,

"——— ———, *Cashier.*"

————◆————

From the Maine Savings Bank, Portland, comes the following :—

One morning a small, ragged and ill-fed Irish boy presented himself, and said he wished to draw twenty-five cents ; he was told that we could not pay him less than a dollar (as per our by-laws) ; he gave his head one or two tremendous digs, and evidently evolved therefrom something, but what ?

Finally he said he would take the dollar, which was accordingly given him and he departed, but only to the front door-steps, where, carefully selecting the brightest quarter of a dollar from the four just given him, he turned and again appeared at the teller's desk, where he said he would deposit seventy-five cents, which he did.

When that young Irish financier presents himself now at the counter for the purpose of drawing money, more or less, that section of the by-laws that says no sums of less than one dollar shall be paid, has no meaning for him.

The future of that little Irish boy will be watched with interest, and if you ever issue volume 2, I have no doubt but what he will furnish another story of his smartness, and which I will report (D. V.).

Fraternally yours,

STEPHEN G. ROGERS, *Treasurer.*

N. B.—An Irish woman once told me she wished to deposit some money for her niece, Michael Hogan.

A dry thing sometimes finds its way to a cashier's desk, as, for instance, this reply to a collection of ours :

"Your draft for mitten bill rec'd ; Mr. Higgle says, 'if you will *o*mit exchange, he will *re*mit as soon as his exchequer will *ad*mit.' *Per*mit me to advise you to *sub*mit to such deduction, and I will re*com*mit to messenger as *com*mittee to collect."

What sort of *ear* must that *ere* cash*ier* have ? Ought he not to be cash*iered* or *e'er* it be too late ? Can he be called a pundit ?

Says another cashier :

Our messenger presenting a draft to a testy resident, was told to "take it to h—l." We were compelled to return it to the sender as unable to collect, having no correspondent in that locality.

SOFT WORDS FOR BANK DIRECTORS.

Several of the directors of the New York Mechanics' and Laborers' Savings Bank (which recently suspended), have received an anonymous letter, introduced by the skull and cross-bones which occupy so conspicuous a place in Molly Maguire literature, and couched in the following language:

"You are hereby warned to make good the money you have stolen, or I will coolly drive a bullet through you. You are worse than the thief that will meet a man in the street and take his money. I could protect myself of the highwayman, but not of you. You are a sneak-thief that will suffer surely if you do not come down with the money. Six days will be given you to think. Beware!"

TO ALL EDITORS OF ALL NEWSPAPERS.

My Dear Gentlemen :—You are extremely kind, but let me entreat you to desist. I am *so* tired. Can't you write about something else besides finance? Please do. Woman is a copious theme, and the weather is always a

7

neat and handy topic. I quite agree with both sides of you. Your arguments are absolutely unanswerable. There ought to be no end of greenbacks and also nothing but gold. Both are a great deal better than either. You have convinced me of this so often that I am in a state of sublime addle. But this is not all. I observe with anguish and alarm that the more you write about finance the less there is of finance. Let me beg you not to write any more. If you do, money will totally disappear. Soon the surface of the globe will be covered with able editorials two feet deep. There will not be a dollar on earth, nor a living man, and the epitaph of the human race will be, "Died of finance on the brain, without a solitary red."

I am, dear gentlemen, your suffering servant,

G. WASH. MEEKINS, M. D.

------♦------

NASBY ON GREENBACKISM.

"This money ain't never to be redeemed. It will go on and on forever. When a bill gets old, yoo kin go and exchange it for a new one, and that for another new one. The people will be obleeged to take it, for it will be legle-tender, and it can't help makin money plenty, wich is wat we want now. Pay! never! Ef we are a goin to pay we mite be benefitted for a time, but it wood be but temprary. We want permanent finanshel relief, suthin that will last. A unlimitid ishoo uv money and a libral system uv internal improvements to git it into cirkelashen is wat we want now."

Issaker was satisfied, and to-morrow nite we meet to organize the "Onlimited Ishoo and Internel Improvement League uv the Cross-Roads."

Our rallying cry will be, "Our capassity for spendin money must be ekel to our capassity for perdoosin it, and both must be onlimited." We shel hev good times at the Corners ez soon ez the Nationals carry a congress, and kin git to work. I hev developed the skeem for em.

PETROLEUM V. NASBY, *Finanseer.*

EX-TREASURER SPINNER.—PLEASANT RECOLLECTIONS OF HIS EARLY LIFE.

[FROM CORRESPONDENCE OF AMSTERDAM, N. Y., DEMOCRAT.]

Frederick E. Spinner was born in the town of Herkimer, some seventy years ago. At the age of seventeen he removed to Amsterdam, and, after a short apprenticeship, entered the harness shop of "Uncle David" DeForest. He worked for him for some time, and then went into partnership, but this was soon dissolved. He was a famous reader during his sojourn in Amsterdam, and could generally be found reclining in some shady nook poring over some literary work. History was his favorite, and he always remembered everything he read. At one time parties sent to an Albany library to learn as

to the correct version of some disputed question, but in
this case, as always, Spinner's never-failing memory was
found to be right. He used to annoy Mr. DeForest
terribly by his habit of sitting up late at night reading,
while "Uncle David" vainly sought to court the ".drowsy
god," until at last "forbearance ceased to be a virtue,"
and a well-aimed pillow would generally put an extin-
guisher upon both the candle and the literary flame.
While here he spent a great deal of time practicing upon
the famous autograph which has figured upon so many
greenbacks, and furnished to quill-drivers an endless
theme for witticisms. Mr. DeForest remembers to have
seen two hundred sheets of foolscap upon which Spinner
had scribbled his inimitable signature. By assiduous
practice he acquired a species of hieroglyphic, which
no forger has ever been found rash enough to wrestle
with. After the dissolution of the partnership with Mr.
DeForest, Mr. Spinner returned to Herkimer, and soon
showed his enterprising nature by advocating the pav-
ing and flagging of the streets, which were then in de-
plorable condition. He carried out the measure in spite
of determined opposition, and the village soon wore a
new and improved aspect. Of this improvement Mr.
Spinner said, that "while it was being carried out no
man in town had so many enemies, but when it was finished no one had so many friends." Soon after Mr.
Spinner was "prominently mentioned" for the position
of Sheriff of Herkimer county ; but a certain old citizen
named Bellinger was determined to have the honor of
the office without any of the duties incumbent upon it.

Consequently, an arrangement was agreed upon by which Bellinger was elected sheriff in name, while Spinner performed all the duties. When the Insane Asylum was being built, Mr. Spinner was one of the overseers of the work, and while engaged in the duty unwittingly gave offense to Gov. Seward, and was soon after allowed a vacation for an indefinite period of time. Presently he was heard from as the Republican candidate for Congress from the Herkimer district, and was triumphantly elected, changing a district usually sure for 1,600 Democratic majority to 1,500 Republican. He served his term in Congress with credit, and at its close applied to President Lincoln for a modest naval berth, but was informed that something better was in store for him, and was soon after appointed Treasurer of the United States. At the close of his term he returned to Mohawk, and there met again the friend and partner of his youthful days, whom he had not seen in fifty-four years. Mr. De Forest recalls, with great satisfaction, this pleasant reunion. Mr. Spinner gave his old friend a hearty welcome, and they spent a happy hour together, living old times over again.

THE OLDEST REPORT.—A FRAGMENT.

The trustees of the first Savings Bank organized in New York watched the general results of the new institution with much interest. After only six months of operation, the first report contained the following encouraging statement, as true now as then :

" He who has learned to be economical has first gotten
rid of pernicious modes of spending money.   Every
time he adds to his amount he has an additional motive
for perseverance.   In the provision he is making for the
future is associated all which can gratify him as a father,
a husband, a guardian or friend.   The talent which
heaven has committed to his care he improves for the
objects of his affection ; this again endears them to him,
and thus the sum of human happiness is increased and
extended.   It is impossible for men continuing to act on
such principles to be immoral.

" The trustees are glad to report, that the habit of
saving among the depositors becomes very soon not only
delightful but permanent.   Those who have brought
their one dollar are anxious to increase it to five, and so
on."

Then follows, in this first Savings Bank report, a
number of practical examples showing plainly enough
the great good the system was destined to accomplish.

————◆————

"Give me six lines of a man's handwriting, and I
can hang him," said Talleyrand, years ago.   Ben Butler
constructed a similar apothegm when he said he would
rather go five hundred miles to see a man, than to write
him a letter ; and yet indiscreet folks will continue to
write dangerous letters that are afterwards found in
trunks and published in the newspapers.

MATTERS OF INTEREST.

A MORTGAGE.

IN the whole range of sacred and profane literature, perhaps there is nothing recorded which has such staying properties as a good healthy mortgage. A mortgage can be depended on to stick closer than a brother. It has a mission to perform which never lets up. Day after day it is right there, nor does the slightest tendency to slumber impair its vigor in the night. Night and day, on the Sabbath, and at holiday times, without a moment's rest for sickness or recreation, the biting offspring of its existence, interest, goes on. The seasons may change, days run into weeks, weeks into months, and months be swallowed up into the gray man of advancing years, but that mortgage stands up in steepful vigilance, with the interest, a perennial stream, ceaselessly running on. Like a huge nightmare eating out the sleep of some restless slumberer, the unpaid mortgage rears up its gaunt front in perpetual torment to the miserable wight who is held within its pitiless clutch. It holds the poor victims with the relentless grasp of a giant ; not one hour of recreation ; not a moment's evasion of its hideous presence. A genial savage of mollifying aspect while the interest is paid ; a very devil of hopeless destruction when the payments fail.

[151]

A CURIOUS PUZZLE.

Here is something to scratch your head over. A very curious number is 142,857, which, multiplied by 1, 2, 3, 4, 5, or 6, gives the same figures in the same order, beginning at a different point, but if multiplied by 7 gives all nines:

$$142,857 \times 1 = 142,857$$
$$142,857 \times 2 = 285,714$$
$$142,857 \times 3 = 428,571$$
$$142,857 \times 4 = 571,428$$
$$142,857 \times 5 = 714,285$$
$$142,857 \times 6 = 857,142$$
$$142,857 \times 7 = 999,999$$

Multiply 142,857 by 8, and you have 1,142,856. Then add the first figure to the last, and you have 142,857, the original number, with figures exactly the same as at the start.

HOW INTEREST EATS.

One dollar, loaned for one hundred years, at 6 per cent., with interest annually collected and added to principal, will amount to $340.

At 8 per cent. it amounts to $2,203, or about seven times as much.

At 3 per cent. it amounts to $19.25.

At 10 per cent. it amounts to $13,809, or seven hundred times as much.

At 12 per cent. it amounts to $84,075, or four thousand times as much.

At 18 per cent. it amounts to $15,145,007 ; and at "two per cent. a month," it yields the enormous sum of $2,551,799,404.

Borrowers will consult this item, and choose such rate as they deem themselves best able to stand. Surely, "he who goes a-borrowing, goes a-sorrowing."

Fifty years use of $100, at 6 per cent., compounded annually, gives the amount of $1,842. And the same, at 8 per cent., is 4,890. And $1,000, compounded annually at 10 per cent., runs up in fifty years to the snug fortune of $117,390.

Lend not beyond thy ability, nor refuse to lend out of thy ability ; especially when it will help others more than it can hurt thee. If thy debtor be honest and capable, thou hast thy money again, if not with increase, with praise. If he prove insolvent, do not ruin him to get that which it will not ruin thee to lose ; for thou art but a steward, and another is thy owner, master and judge.

WILLIAM PENN.

COMPOUND INTEREST.

It has been supposed here that had America been purchased in 1607 for $1, and payment secured by bond, payable, with interest annually compounded, in

7*

1876 at 10 per cent., the amount would be—I have not verified the calculation—the very snug little sum of $136,000,000,000 ; five times as much as the country will sell for to-day.   Capt. Smith or Newport, whichever it was, has therefore been ruined, or would have been, if he had run in debt a dollar for this continent.

It is very much like supposing that if Adam and Eve had continued to multiply and replenish once in two years until the present time, and all their descendants had lived and had been equally prolific, then, saying nothing about twins and triplets, there would now be actually alive upon the earth a quantity of human beings in solid measure more than thirteen and one-fourth times the bulk of the entire planet ; and if all these people had been thrifty, and saved one cent a year and invested it at 10 per cent. compound interest, the amount in currency at eighty-eight cents in gold would buy not only all the real estate there is in this world, but ten times as much as there is in the universe, at double the government price for public lands, and leave enough to do the entire sewerage for the main streets connecting the fixed stars, and to pave the milky way with well-cut diamonds of the first water, nine feet cube, three thousand miles wide (including sidewalks to be made of condensed rainbows, three billions to the square yard), and a distance of 996,834,329,648,196,314,983 thousand million billion trillion miles long.   And I believe there would be considerable left in bank even then.

—*Speech in Congress.*

BEST INTEREST RULE.

FOR TWELVE PER CENT.

Multiply the principal by one-third the number of days, thus : (Decimal points omitted.)

$$
\begin{array}{lll}
\text{For 34 days, multiply by} & .11\tfrac{1}{3} \\
\quad\ 64 \quad\text{``}\quad\quad\text{``}\quad\quad\text{``} & .21\tfrac{1}{3} \\
\quad\ 94 \quad\text{``}\quad\quad\text{``}\quad\quad\text{``} & .31\tfrac{1}{3}
\end{array}
$$

FOR NINE PER CENT.

Multiply the principal by one-fourth the number of days, thus :

$$
\begin{array}{lll}
\text{For 34 days, multiply by} & .85 \\
\quad\ 64 \quad\text{``}\quad\quad\text{``}\quad\quad\text{``} & .16 \\
\quad\ 94 \quad\text{``}\quad\quad\text{``}\quad\quad\text{``} & .235
\end{array}
$$

For other notes, take fractional parts of result by above rules.

FOR EXAMPLE :

Find Interest 64 days on $840, at 12 per cent.

$$
\begin{array}{lll}
840 = & \text{product by} & 1 \\
1680 = & \text{`} \quad\quad\text{``} & 2 \\
18 = & \text{``}\quad\quad\text{``} & \tfrac{1}{3} \\
\hline
\$17.92 = & \text{``}\quad\quad\text{``} & 21\tfrac{1}{3} \quad \text{Ans.}
\end{array}
$$

ONE THING THAT AN APE CAN DO.

The Siamese ape is stated to be in great request among native merchants as a cashier in their counting-houses. Vast quantities of base coin obtain circulation in Siam, and the faculty of discriminating between good money and bad appears to be possessed by these gifted monkeys in such an extraordinary degree of development that no human being, however carefully trained, can compete with them. The cashier ape puts into his mouth each coin presented to him in business payments, and tests it with grave deliberation. If it be genuine, he hands it to his master ; if counterfeit, he sets it down before him with a solemn grimace of displeasure. His method of testing is regarded in commercial circles as infallible.

EIGHT PER CENT. PER MONTH.

A singular instance of human credulity is reported from Munich. The actress, Adele Spitzeder, who was sentenced there about six years ago to a term of imprisonment for having swindled the public out of many millions by her banking institution, the Dachauer Banken, conducted, as she asserted, for the furtherance of the interests of the Roman Catholic religion, tried again after her liberation from prison to earn a living on the stage. Finding that this could not be done, she has returned to Munich and again opened a bank. Deposits, on which she pays eight per cent. monthly interest, are brought to her in abundance, and, of course, another catastrophe will occur in time.

FIAT MONEY.

During the fierce and universal discussion of the "unlimited greenback" question, which so recently disturbed everybody, the absurdities of an unredeemable currency were well put in a few tons of Fiat Money. We have heard of no banks issuing that particular kind of money, but some thousands of people were earnest advocates of a circulation very like it.

WORTH REMEMBERING.

The advantages of Savings Banks to depositors and their families cannot be fitly described in words. For who can measure the want and suffering relieved in dark days of trouble—the increased industry, thrift and independence which the habit of saving promotes—how much temptation to idleness, sensual indulgence, vice and crime prevented—how much greater the pay, and much steadier the demand for the superior and reliable labor or services of a sober, intelligent and sturdy workman—how the standard of thrift and economy in wife and daughters is raised—how much more decent and decorous in dress and manner all the members of the family—how they rise, insensibly to themselves, it may be, in the respect and confidence of the best classes in their neighborhood—how much oftener in church or lecture-room or at the circulating library—how much prompter at school, and how marvelous the progress—

how all the blessings of this life cluster around such a household—how happy marriages, future honors, fortune,. friends, usefulness, happiness greet the manhood and womanhood of the Savings Bank depositor's children when his work is over—and how brighter the prospect for such a family when their serious thoughts stretch off to the life to come.—*B. R. in the Safeguard*, 1874.

USURY AND INTEREST.

The word "Interest" appears first in an act of Parliament of the 21st James I., 1623, wherein it was made to signify a lawful increase by way of compensation for money lent. The rate fixed by the act was £8 for the use of £100 for a year, in place of usury at £10, before taken. The rate was lowered to £6 in 1650 ; and by an act of the 13th of Queen Anne, 1713, it was reduced to £5. The restraint being found prejudicial to commerce, it was totally removed by Victoria (1854). Until the 15th century, no Christians were allowed to receive interest on money, and Jews were the only usurers, and therefore often banished and persecuted. In 1262 there were 700 Jews slain in London—a Jew having forced a Christian to pay him more than 2s. per week, as interest on a loan of 20s. In 1274, every Jew lending money on interest was compelled to wear a plate on his breast, signifying that he was a usurer, or quit the realm ; and four years later 267 Jews were hanged and quartered for clipping English coin.

COUNTERFEITS AND ROGUES.

ORIENTAL BOGUS.

An ingenious case of counterfeiting coin was recently discovered at Hoshungabad, in India. Natives, when testing mohurs, or other gold coin, generally take them to a jeweler to have a hole drilled half way through them, for the purpose of seeing that they are of genuine metal. The coiner, a jeweler by trade, manufactured silver imitations of gold mohurs, and having drilled two or three holes half way through them, to make it appear that they had been as often tested, thickly gilded them over. By these means he for some time imposed even on members of his own craft, till one, more wily than the others, proceeded to test some of the counterfeit coins for himself.

A CLEVER CHEAT.

[HOW A SIMPLE-HEARTED MAN WAS TAKEN IN.]

In Francis' "History of the Bank of England" the following story is told:

In 1780 a gentleman of eminence in the mercantile world was grieved by the contents of a letter which he received from a correspondent at Hamburg, the postmark of which it bore. From the statement it contained, it appears that a person, most minutely described, had defrauded the writer under extraordinary circumstances, of £3,000. The letter continued to say information had been obtained that the defrauder—the dress and person of whom it described—was occasionally to be seen at the Dutch Walk of the Royal Exchange. The object of the writer was to inform his correspondent to invite the party to dinner, and, by any moral force which could be used, compel him to return the money, adding that, if he should be found amenable to reason, and evince any signs of repentance, he might be dismissed with a friendly caution and £500, as he was a near relative of the writer. As the gentleman whose name it bore was a profitable correspondent, the London merchant kept a keen watch on the Dutch Walk, and was at last successful in meeting and being introduced to the cheat.

The invitation to dine was accepted, and the host, having previously given notice to his family to quit the table soon after dinner, acquainted the visitor with his knowledge of the fraud. Alarm and horror were depicted in the countenance of the young man, who, with tones apparently tremulous from emotion, begged that his disgrace might not be made public. To this the merchant consented, provided the £3,000 were returned. The visitor sighed deeply, but said that to return all was impossible, as he had unfortunately spent part of the amount. The remainder, however, he proposed to yield instantly, and the notes were handed to the merchant, who, after dilating on the goodness of the man he had robbed, concluded his moral lesson by handing over a check for £500, as a proof of his beneficence. The following morning the gentleman went to the banker to deposit the money he had received, when, to his great surprise, he was told that the notes were counterfeit. His next inquiries were concerning the check, but that had been cashed shortly after the opening of the bank. He immediately sent an express to his Hamburg correspondent, who replied that the letter was a forgery, and that no fraud had been committed upon him. The whole affair had been plotted by a gang, some of whom were on the Continent and some in England.

A PLUCKY CASHIER.

PITTSBURGH, PA., *April* 30, 1878.—A bold but unsuccessful attempt was made to-day to rob the Workingmen's Savings Bank, on Ohio street, Alleghany. The book-keeper of the bank had gone to dinner, leaving the cashier, George L. Walker, alone. Two men entered the bank and one of them, advancing to the rear counter, asked silver for a dollar bill, and when the cashier advanced with the change in his hand, he was confronted with a cocked revolver and told to make no noise or he would be shot. Dropping the silver, Walker seized the revolver and succeeded in wrenching it from his assailants, who then clambered up and got inside and were reaching for money on the counter when Walker opened fire on him, firing two shots at him and also two at the other robber, who in the meantime had climbed over the front counter and was advancing to the rear of the room. The strangers were dismayed by their warlike reception and then fled and have not yet been arrested. The bank sustained no loss.

A CLEVER SWINDLE.

A young man named E. J. Murphy called on the banking house of Henry Clews & Co., New York, a week ago and inquired about the price of bonds. Monday he called again and bought two $1,000 four per cent. coupon bonds and one $500 four per cent. bond. He gave in payment a draft for $2,540, drawn by the Commercial National Bank of Chicago on the Bank of New York, dated February 27, 1879, payable to the order of Henry Clews & Co. The firm sent the draft to the Bank of New York for an indorsement of the certification. The teller said it was all right, and Murphy carried off his bonds. Tuesday the clearing-house sent back the draft as all wrong. It was originally a draft for $254, but a cipher had been added and the date changed. A reward of $1,000 has been offered for Murphy's capture.

BOLD ROBBERY IN A BANK.

A very bold robbery was committed yesterday afternoon at the Mechanics' Bank, corner of Fulton and

Montague streets, Brooklyn. It seems that Mr. A. H. Howe, a coal and wood dealer, entered the bank for the purpose of depositing $362 in bills. After counting the money, he approached the teller's desk, and laying the money on the little glass slab in front, placed his account-book on it. His right hand rested on the book. While Mr. Howe stood waiting for the teller, who was engaged, a man approached, and, standing close to his left shoulder, held out a check on the Long Island Bank, asking at the same time if Mr. Howe knew where the bank was. The latter was about to give the information when he felt something whiz by his left ear, and in almost the same instant the stranger who had asked him about the check disappeared through the bank door. Turning to the little window in front of the teller Mr. Howe was dumbfounded to find—although his hand still rested on his account book, and he had not felt any disturbance—that the money was gone. When he recovered from his astonishment sufficiently to tell the bank officers that he had been robbed, it was too late to pursue the thief or thieves, if there were more than one. The police are making every effort in the matter, but have very little in the way of a clue to start on.

———•———

Yochantsoff, cashier of the Credit Foncier Bank, of St. Petersburg, has been arrested as a defaulter to the amount of $1,375,000. It is gratifying to know that defalcation is not exclusively confined to this country.

THE HEATHEN CHINEE.

It is said that the Chinaman is incapable of civilization. Facts disprove this assertion. Ah Chung had been working in San Gabriel, Cal., and received a check for $151. The figures were raised by Chung to $951, and the amount was paid on demand at the Farmers' and Merchants' Bank of Los Angeles. No trace of the Chinaman has since been discovered.

DISGUSTED WITH MEN.

A well known bank president said, on hearing of the great bank robbery at Northampton :

"I'm sick of this rascally world. Don't want to see or do business with anybody. I'd rather be an old farmer, living on a cross-road, four miles from the sight of everybody, with a barrel of cider and two hogs, than to have anything to do with banks, money or men."

DOGS PREFERRED.

Said a Richmond bank president, while examining a lot of finely-executed counterfeit currency, "What a world of rascals this is, to be sure ! The more I see of *men* and learn of their damnable villainy, the more profound respect and love I have for *dogs !* "

A ROUSING BURGLARY.

[HOW AN ENTERPRISING BUT IMPRUDENT TRIO WAKED UP FISHKILL
LANDING.]

The pretty little village of Fishkill Landing, on the
Hudson, was awakened by a great crash at about 2.30
o'clock yesterday morning, which brought the inhabitants to their windows and to the streets in a twinkling.
They saw great quantities of smoke issuing from the
counting-room of the First National Bank—so thick
that for a few moments no one could enter the bank.
When it cleared away a few of the villagers went in, and
found almost complete ruin. Burglars had been at
work, and in trying to open a safe with powder had
literally blown it to pieces. The glass in the front window of the bank was all blown out, and some fragments
were thrown seventy-five feet across the road, landing
on the piazza of the Revere House opposite. The contents of the safe were thrown about in wild confusion ;
books, papers, and pieces of discolored silver plate and
coin covered the floor.

Adjoining the banking-room, and separated from it
by only a thin partition, through which there is commu-
nication by an ordinary pine door, are the law offices of
Mr. John F. Schlosser, Jr. The outer door of this office
had been forced by a jimmy, and so the burglars gained
admission to the bank. Two safes stood before them ;
one a new Herring safe, fire and burglar proof, and the
other a safe which had been called fire and burglar proof

about fifteen years ago, before safe robbers became so expert as some safe robbers are, and some are not, now. The thieves selected the old safe, which contained only the books of the bank, some valuable papers that had been left by the bank's customers for safe-keeping, some silverware, about $70 worth of foreign coin, and nearly $60 in cents and five-cent pieces.

There is much speculation as to who were the bold but comic burglars. During the day three strangers entered the bank half a dozen times, and were persistent in their efforts to sell a pair of daubs of oil paintings. They stayed several minutes each time, would not take "no" for an answer, and insisted upon having some one make them an offer, and it is thought possible that during these visits they were watching the clerks, and taking a survey of the interior of the bank.

—*New York World, Oct.* 11, 1878.

A REMARKABLE COUNTERFEIT.

"The sub-Treasury Department at New Orleans have come across a counterfeit silver quarter, a remarkable feature about which is, that it is intrinsically more valuable than the genuine quarter dollar. According to Mr. M. V. Davis, the efficient coiner at the Mint, to whom it was sent to be assayed, it weighs 978 grains, or 135 above legal weight, and contains 50 millimes of silver above standard, also three millimes of gold, which silver coins do not contain, except in rare instances. Mr. James

Albrecht, the assayer, reports that its fineness is .950 silver, and .003 gold. The only defect in the piece is in the engraving of the words, 'In God we trust.' The word 'America' is abbreviated to 'Amea.,' in the words, 'United States America.'"

A DANGEROUS BANK-NOTE.

It is probable that Burns vastly exaggerated the advantages of seeing ourselves as others see us. The vision is often amusing, but it is not always strictly veracious. Other people and other nations, though they may possess a gift of superior impartiality, sometimes lack the necessary information, and on such occasions the default is made up by the historic use of the imagination. It may be safely said, however, that our own view of ourselves is scarcely so diverting as that of foreigners. English history, for example, to be really comic, should be written by the *feuilletonist* of a Paris journal, and the essays of the late Gilbert a'Beckett in caricature-chronicle labored in vain by the side of the works of these humorous students of British manners and customs. It would be worth the while of some careful editor like Mr. Timbs to collect in a volume the many curious things that have been said of us by our French neighbors, and certainly they would well deserve the title of "things not generally known." The latest contribution to this interesting branch of literature relates a highly important fact with regard to the Duke of Richmond. It is said that among the possessions he inherited from the late duke was found a bank-note for £50,000. This unique piece of paper money, of whose existence we have no doubt, was preserved with great caution, and by means which must have been a source of peril to friends and foes. We are informed that the late duke caused the note to be deposited in a casket, and this casket was so fastened that any one who attempted to handle it at once received six pistol-shots. The ingenious casket, we are told, became a burdensome possession to the present duke. His ancestor had not transmitted to him the secret by which it might be opened with safety, and he was, therefore, not unnaturally, timid in the examination of his treasure. Under these circumstances, we are not surprised to learn that he finally determined to deliver the casket and its contents to the Bank of England, and to permit the officers of that establishment to investigate the ingenuity of the terrible contrivance. The duties of property would even be in excess of its rights if every inheritance were "tied up" in this way.

PRECOCITY.

Forgery is becoming so fashionable that even the children engage in it. In Geneva, New York, a youth of sixteen forged his father's name, recently, to a check for $1,024, and drawing the money ran away to New York to spend it. After his money was all spent he was arrested, and held to await the arrival of his father, who telegraphed instructions to detain him. The father ought to invent a more difficult signature, or have the boy locked up.

very respectfully yours

R. M. Buckle

HISTORICAL MEMORANDA.

A VETERAN CASHIER.

[SEE FRONTISPIECE.]

THE present cashier of the National Union Bank of Maryland (Baltimore), ROBERT MICKLE, Esq., is believed to be the oldest bank officer in the United States. Born July 1, 1798, he entered the service of the Union Bank of Maryland in September, 1819, as discount clerk, and in 1830 was appointed cashier, which position he has held until the present time. So rare an instance of faithful service in one bank is well worthy of permanent record. During his sixty years of banking life, what changes and rare experiences he has witnessed. How few of his early customers are living to-day! How changed the financial affairs of the country! Mr. Mickle is yet hale and vigorous, apparently good for another decade or more of cashiership, which the Scrap-Book devoutly hopes he may be spared to enjoy, until

" ——like a clock worn out with eating time
The wheels of weary life at last stand still."

8   [169]

Another case of long-continued service in one bank, which perhaps is almost equally remarkable, is that of William H. Foster, Esq., the present cashier of the Asiatic National Bank, Salem, Mass., who commenced as book-keeper *in that bank* in May, 1824, and since December, 1834, has been its efficient and faithful cashier.

———◆———

HON. JOHN SHERMAN,

SECRETARY OF THE TREASURY.

The Hon. John Sherman, secretary of the treasury, was born in Lancaster, Ohio, May 10, 1823. He is one of a large family of children, another of whom is Gen. W. T. Sherman, and his father was Charles T. Sherman, at that time judge of the supreme court of the State. He was educated for the law, and in 1844 was admitted to the bar and practiced in his native State. In 1848 he was a delegate to the Whig National Convention which met in Philadelphia, June 7, and nominated Zachary Taylor for president, and Millard Fillmore for vice-president, and in 1852 he was a delegate to the Baltimore Convention of the same party, which nominated General Winfield Scott and Wm. A. Graham, of North Carolina, for the respective offices. Mr. Sherman was elected in 1854 to the thirty-fourth congress, and re-elected in 1856 and 1858. In the thirty-sixth congress (1858) he was selected by the republican party, as candidate for speaker. He was again chosen in 1860 as a member of the thirty-seventh congress, but in 1861 Hon. Salmon P.

Chase resigned the Senatorship from Ohio to become
Mr. Lincoln's secretary of the treasury, and Mr. Sherman
was elected to fill the vacant chair. He was at once
made a member of the committee on finance, and in 1864
was made its chairman, and so continued while he remained in the senate. He also served on the judiciary
and Pacific R. R. committees. In 1867 he was re-elected,
and he received a similar indorsement at the hands of
his fellow-citizens in 1873.

Senator Sherman gave an earnest support to the war
measures of Mr. Lincoln's cabinet, and his thorough practical acquaintance with financial matters was of great
service to the government, as, from his position at the head
of the finance committee, which he retained throughout,
he was enabled to co-operate actively in all the great
financial measures necessitated by the war. On the
accession to office of President Hayes, March 4, 1877, Mr.
Sherman was presented with the portfolio of secretary
of the treasury, and the fitness of the appointment was
universally recognized. Under his administration many
important financial measures have been carried out, the
greenback dollar has been brought to par with gold, the
national debt has been reduced by many millions, and
the refunding of much of the debt at four and four and
one-half per cent. has effected an annual saving in interest of many millions more. The act for the resumption
of specie payments had no more resolute champion than
the subject of this brief sketch, and it is not too much to
say that his financial policy, at once progressive and
conservative, has inspired respect and confidence in

American government securities on every exchange and bourse in the civilized world.

—*Chicago Bankers' Directory.*

———·———

A NEW ENGLAND CASHIER of many years' experience sends us a page as below. The Suffolk Bank item will hit a familiar spot in the memory of the older bank people. Happily, our almost perfect National Bank currency has done away with such little tricks.

HOW THE SUFFOLK BANK WAS BEATEN AT ITS OWN GAME.

In the early days of New England banks, when their notes were redeemed only at their own counters, the Boston merchants were much exercised over the discount they were compelled to pay on the notes of the country banks which they were obliged to take from their customers.

To obviate this difficulty, the Suffolk Bank was conceived and organized, and the New England banks, out of Boston, were very pleasantly invited to deposit funds with that bank for the redemption of their notes. If the officers of any bank failed to accept the invitation, they found, some fine day, a representative of the Suffolk Bank at their counter, with a pile of their notes, and a polite request that they might be converted into specie.*

* NOTE.—This system, introduced by the Suffolk Bank, is the foundation of the present system of redemption for the National Banks, with a Central Bureau at Washington.

If the first call did not bring them into subjection, the second or third was pretty sure to, and deter others from following their example, though I believe there were one or two intractables.

There were, at that time, but two banks in the city of Hartford—the Hartford and the Phœnix Banks, with capital of about a million and a quarter dollars each. They were willing to redeem their notes in Boston, but were not willing to keep a balance on deposit for that purpose, as the Suffolk Bank required.

I have heard the late Mr. George Beach, then, and for many years after, cashier, and subsequently president of the Phœnix Bank—a sound financier and a noble man—relate the attempt of the Suffolk Bank to compel them to accede to its terms.

There appeared, one day, at the bank in Hartford, a messenger from the Suffolk Bank, with a large package of their notes, and demanded the specie. (This was in the days of the stage-coach, when railroads were not.)

Mr. Beach, in anticipation of this visit, had provided himself, from New York, with drafts on the Suffolk to a large amount. So, leaving the president and teller to pay out the specie to the Suffolk man, he started at once for Boston, to present his drafts before the messenger could return as a reinforcement. Arrived in due time, he walked into the bank and presented to the teller a draft for $5,000, which was promptly paid in coin, when he presented a second draft for a like amount. In those primitive days, a curtain behind the counter, dividing the room, served to form the directors' room. While the teller was paying the second draft, first one person and then another stepped from behind the curtain, looked, and then stepped back again.

That draft being paid, he presented a third, for a larger amount. This was followed by a slight commotion behind the curtain, and a prolonged, low whistle gave evidence that the shot told pretty effectually.

He was finally invited into the " directors' room ;" and after convincing the gentlemen present that he was still well supplied with ammunition, a truce was asked, resulting in an agreement that the Hartford banks might redeem their notes in Boston in their own way.

Our bank (then a State bank) at one time had some small bills printed on thin paper, which proved to be of bad quality, doing but poor service. An Irishman presented one of them, from which a third or more was gone, for redemption. I asked him what had become of the other part. " Sorra a bit do I know, your honor," said he, " an' I think it must have milted."

A countryman came into the bank one day to buy a draft to send to a woman, giving her name. Wishing to put a handle to her name, he was asked if she were Miss, or Mrs. After considering the question a moment, he replied, " Oh, Miss ; she is a widow."

THE NEWSBOYS' SAVINGS BANK.

That admirable charity, the Children's Aid Society of New York, has a banking curiosity worth noticing, at the Newsboys' Lodging House, corner of Duane and New Chambers street. It is a bank for the newsboys—a penny bank on a large scale, and is quite unique. It has no books, no stationery, no safe, no directors' meetings; and though carried on for twenty-five years winding up its affairs and beginning anew every month, and paying the ruinous interest of *five per cent. per month* to all depositors, there have been no losses, no failures and no embezzlements. Nothing, however, could be simpler or more practical. A heavy oak table by the superintendent's desk in the large assembly room, containing 150 or more boxes—one for each lodger—and a metal cover with a narrow opening for coin over each box, numbered to correspond with the depositor's register number, constitutes about all the machinery. The only "Rules and Regulations" are—Deposit any amount you please, and all money returned at end of the month with five per cent. interest added. The bank open for payments on last day of the month only. This Savings Bank is a most valuable contrivance, and one which has materially aided many boys in forming habits of thrift.

About $3,000 is now deposited every year, the total amount for twenty-five years being $44,909.13. Many of the boys deposit their monthly pile in the city Savings Banks, and quite a number have thus accumulated several hundred dollars as a fund to start in life with ; while thousands of these little waifs, all ready to become vagrants and tramps, have been taught by this little bank how to become self-sustaining citizens. All honor to the wise, benevolent founders of the Newsboys' Bank !

MAKING DEPOSITS IN THE NEWSBOYS' BANK.

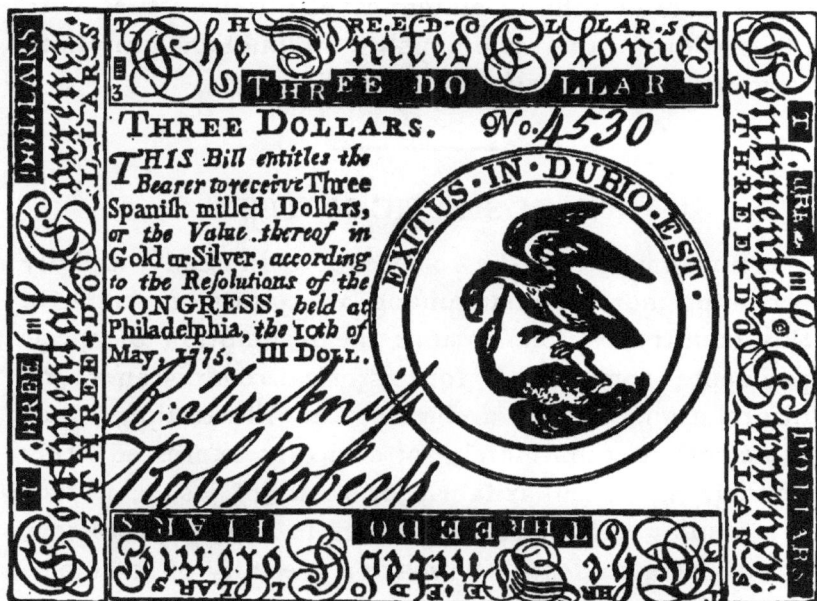

DOLLARS OF THE DADDIES.

The Bank Notes of our forefathers were very different looking affairs to the present beautiful specimens of engraving furnished us by the Government, as will be seen by the above engraving. They were printed upon coarse brown paper (having silk fiber in it, similar to that in use now). All the States issued paper money, similar in appearance, but different in general design, and evinced a singular unanimity in repudiating their issues when the time for payment arrived, Vermont alone (not then admitted into the Union) redeeming its

8*

entire issue in gold.   Catalogues of all the issues, with
illustrations of the various notes, are published in cheap
form for the information of the curious.

————————

NUMISMATIC NOTES.

Numismatics, or the science of coin study, is daily
becoming more popular among all classes of people in
this country, especially since the resumption of specie
payment ; some use it for historical reminiscence and
information, or for archæological illustration, while
some collect coins merely for curiosity, expressed either
in their age, peculiar fabric, or rarity of issue ; in fact,
it is similar to most other sciences in this respect—they
always have students who make a specialty of some particular branch.

Coins furnish us with history which otherwise would
remain buried with the nations we had no record of, as
in the case of the Bactrian series of coins discovered a
few years ago, which revealed to us the fact that a Greek
Empire had existed in Central Asia, of which we knew
nothing until the coins were unearthed.

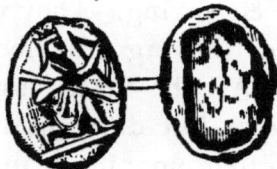

Our illustration is of the Persian Daric, about 520 B.
C., one of the earliest known gold and silver coins ; they

were made by placing a lump of the metal on a die, and a punch used to drive the metal into the design, the punch-mark being the only reverse for the coin ; the obverse represents the Persian conqueror of the Colonial Greeks, Darius Hystaspes (by whom these were struck) kneeling with a bow and arrow. These pieces are rarely found. The metal being so pure, they soon wore smooth, leaving no trace of design. A few are occasionally offered for sale by dealers.

. This cut represents a very early Tetradrachm (or six-drachm piece) of Athens, time of Pericles, about 470 B. C., a coin which circulated in a greater number of countries than any other money of the ancients. They are of fine silver, sometimes quarter inch thick, and in consequence vary much in circumference. Although 2,300 years old, these pieces can often be purchased of coin dealers for $5 or $10, but *rare* varieties sell much higher. The obverse design is the helmeted head of the Goddess Minerva, the local deity ; on the reverse is an owl and a sprig of olive, both sacred to Minerva, probably because they were produced in abundance in the vicinity of Athens. The letters ΑΘΕ indicate the name of the city.

This is a coin of great historical value, a copper shekel of Simon (Son of Gioras), the last prince and defender of Jerusalem, who was defeated and captured by the Roman Emperor Titus, at the destruction of Jerusalem ; carried to Rome and exhibited in the Temple of Jupiter Capitolinus, then executed near the Forum. The obverse bears a palm tree with bunches of dates hanging from the branches, "SIMON," in Hebrew characters ; reverse, a vine leaf and inscription, " *The deliverance of Jerusalem, year first.*" This, being struck in 70 A. D., is consequently the last coin made under Jewish authority. A very fine specimen has lately been brought to this country.

Many numismatists collect only the United States coins ; of these, they endeavor to make a complete series ; scarce dates, being difficult to obtain, sell for high prices when in a fine state of preservation. Many cashiers add considerable to their income by stopping them in circulation and selling them to coin dealers.

SAVINGS BANKS IN EUROPE.

Savings Banks are more numerous and prosperous in Great Britain than in any other European country. Such was the rapid growth of the banks after Parliament made them a subject of legislative action in 1817, that the total amount of deposits in the United Kingdom was, in 1829, nearly fourteen and a half million pounds; and in 1858 there were over one million depositors, and thirty-six million pounds on deposit; and at the present time the number of depositors is more than one and a half million, and the amount of deposits forty-one million pounds, or nearly two hundred million dollars. The Post-Office Savings Banks, organized in 1863, had in 1878 on deposit £28,740,757.

A BIG MONEY-CHEST.

The Bank of England covers five acres, and employs nine hundred clerks. It has no windows opening on the street. Light is admitted through open courts. No mob can take the bank, therefore, without cannon to batter the immense walls. The big clock in the center has fifty dials. Large cisterns are sunk in the inner court, and engines, in perfect order, are always ready in case of fire. The bank was incorporated in 1694. Capital, $90,000,000.

SMALL SAVINGS AND GREAT RESULTS.

When everybody was speculating on the bankruptcy of France at the close of the war, and nobody could see how or where she could borrow a thousand millions of dollars, she simply solved the problem by drawing her own capital from her foreign Savings Banks, paying the exorbitant claims of Germany, and preserving the country from ruin. The small savings which the frugal people of France had been hoarding in foreign Savings Banks for a quarter of a century, constituted the real reserve force which drove the German invader from the soil. This capital stock, chiefly belonging to her hardworking citizens, was the only power that Von Moltke and the "Man of Blood and Iron" were unable to resist.

OLDEST BILL OF EXCHANGE IN THE WORLD.
1325.

The oldest copy of a formal bill of exchange known to be in existence at present, is one dated at Milan, on the 9th of March, 1325, and runs in the original as follows :

"Pagate per questa prima litera (lettera) a di IX Ottobre a Luca do Goro, Lib. XLV. Sono per la valuta qui da Marco Reno, al tempo il pagate e poncte a mió conto e R. che Christo vi guarde Bouromeo de Bouromei de Milano, IX. de Marzo, 1325." Or, in English—

" Pay for this first bill of exchange, on the 9th of October, to Luca Goro, 45 livres : they are for value received here from Marco Reno : at the time of maturity pay the same to my account thanking you, may Christ protect you, Bouromeo de Bouromei of Milan, the 9th of March, 1325."

----◆----

UNCLAIMED DEPOSITS.

The popular impression that old savings banks hold enormous amounts of unclaimed deposits is quite erroneous. The president of the Bowery Savings Bank, which holds deposits of over $30,000,000, and which has been in operation for forty-five years, testifies that the total amount so held in his institution is only $14,900 ; while in all the New York savings banks, with, say $250,000,000 deposits, the total amount unclaimed for twenty years is reported to the State superintendent as but $316,000.

----◆----

THE WORLD'S GREATEST BANKER.

Mayer Anselm Rothschild, the German banker, whose name and fame are world-wide, has done and said a thousand things worthy a place in history.

From his humble Jewish origin he rapidly rose to distinction by his integrity and financial ability, until, in 1806, William, Elector of Hesse, during the French invasion of his States, deposited with this princely banker about $5,000,000 for eight years, without interest. The house of Rothschild, however, paid two per cent. per annum upon the deposit, and in 1823 repaid the entire principal. The wise handling of this immense sum was the source of the colossal fortune of the Rothschilds.

On one occasion, to Sir Thomas Buxton, in England, he said, "My success has always turned upon one maxim. I said, '*I* can do what *another* man can,' and so I am a match for all the rest of 'em. Another advantage I had : I was always an off-hand man. I made a bargain at once. When I was settled in London, the East India Company had £800,000 in gold to sell. I went to the sale and bought the whole of it. I knew the Duke of Wellington *must* have it. I had bought a great many of his bills at a discount. The government sent for me, and *said* they must have it. When they had got it, they didn't know how to get it to Portugal, where they wanted it. I undertook all that, and I sent it through France ; and that was the best business I ever did in my life.

"It requires a great deal of boldness and a great deal of caution to make a great fortune, and when you have got it, it requires ten times as much wit to keep it. If I were to listen to one-half the projects proposed to me, I should ruin myself very soon.

"One of my neighbors is a very ill-tempered man. He tries to vex me, and has built a great place for swine close to my walk. So when I go out I hear first 'grunt, grunt,' then 'squeak, squeak.' But this does me no harm. I am always in good-humor. Sometimes, to amuse myself, I give a beggar a guinea. He thinks it is a mistake, and for fear I should find it out, he runs away as hard as he can. I advise you to give a beggar a guinea sometimes—it is very amusing."

———•———

ORIGIN OF SAVINGS BANKS.

Savings banks are a modern institution. The first is claimed to have been founded at Hamburg in 1778, but it is believed the first regularly chartered bank for savings was organized in 1804, at Tottenham High Cross, the nucleus thereof being the "Friendly Society for the benefit of Women and Children," established five or six years previously by Mrs. Priscilla Wakefield. In 1806, the Provident Institution of London was started. In 1810, Rev. Henry Duncan, minister at Ruthwell, Dumfriesshire, formed the first savings bank in Scotland, and mainly through his efforts the Edinburgh Savings Bank was established in 1814. Dr. Duncan is claimed as the *founder* of savings banks, because he devoted an immense amount of time to their establishment, originating and organizing the first self-sustaining bank, and so arranging his scheme as to make it applicable to the whole country. The government of Great Britain first recognized these institutions in 1817. The first savings bank in America was the Provident Institution for Savings, Boston, chartered December 13, 1816; deposits now, $18,-647,754. Next came the Savings Bank of Baltimore, chartered December, 1818; deposits now, $12,633,162: and the Philadelphia Savings Fund Society, incorporated February 25, 1819, whose deposits now are $14,446,-207.72, belonging to 56,000 depositors.

———◆———

BRIEF EXPLANATION OF BANKING.

Old Mr. Lefevre, father of the former speaker of the House of Commons, and the principal founder of the house of Curries & Co., illustrated the simple theory of banking to a customer one day, in a manner rivaling the best treatises on that subject. The customer in question was one of those men who find it very convenient to have bad memories, and very tantalizing at times to have good ones. His account was almost always overdrawn, and whenever spoken to on the hitch thus occasioned, his answer was invariably the same—he really had forgotten *how* it stood. At last Mr. Lefevre watched his opportunity, caught him one day at the counter, and said to him :

"Mr. Y——, you and I must understand one another something better than we now seem to. I am afraid you don't know what banking really is; give me leave to tell you. It's my business to take care of *your* money ; but I find you are always taking care of *mine*. Now, that is not banking, Mr. Y—— ; it must be the other way. *I'm* the banker, not you. You understand me now, Mr. Y——, I'm sure you do !"

———◆———

THE UNITED STATES MINT.

The United States Mint was established at Philadelphia by Act of Congress, April 2, 1792.

The first money coined was copper cents, in 1793. Silver dollars were first struck in 1794, and the gold eagle in 1795. Up to 1816, the work was done by hand or horse power.

The original building was on Seventh street above Market. The present marble fire-proof structure on Chestnut street, below Broad, was completed in 1833.

The mint is open to visitors daily (except Sundays) from 9 to 12 o'clock, A. M.

Most of the gold now received here comes from Montana Territory, the California gold being mostly sent to the branch Mint at San Francisco. Other branch Mints have been established at Carson City, Nevada, and Denver, Colorado. There are also assay offices at New York, Boise City, Idaho, and Charlotte, N. C. A number of private issues of coin have appeared in various parts of the country, notably from the Bechtler private mint at Rutherfordton, N. C., the "Templeton Reid" mint in Georgia, and later in California, and several private companies in California.

The principal rooms open to visitors are the deposit or weighing room, where all the precious metals are received and weighed, the deposit melting room, where the metal is brought in locked iron boxes after being weighed, and is here mixed with borax and melted, the office of the melter and refiner, the assay rooms, the rolling room—where a number of sets of " rollers " driven by steam, in which the metal strips are reduced to the coin thickness, are noisily working—and the coining room, the most interesting to visitors. In this room are the beautiful, powerful coining presses, each of the ten machines capable of producing one hundred and twenty coins per minute, though seldom run at that rate, the average work being about eighty per minute. The press stamps both sides of the coin with a pressure of from twenty to eighty tons at each revolution. They are attended by ladies. In the second story is the cabinet. Here are to be seen specimen coins of all the nations of the world ; the " widow's mite " of the New Testament, coins of ancient Greece and Rome, and a very fine collection of Chinese and Japanese coins ; also hundreds of medals commemorating important events of nations and individuals. The present superintendent is Hon. A. Loudon Snowden.   P.

THE NEW YORK CLEARING-HOUSE.

The banks of New York city have made their daily exchanges through the New York Clearing House for twenty-six years. Previous to 1853, each bank exchanged checks by sending its porter the entire round of the banks, which tedious process consumed the best part of the day, and was a source of great annoyance in many ways, as well as of speculative tricks on the part of the

NEW YORK CLEARING HOUSE.
MAKING THE ENTIRE DAILY BANK EXCHANGES IN SIX MINUTES.—*Page* 188.

weaker banks, many of which, by the Friday settlement plan, managed to carry a credit of $2,000 or $3,000 with each of thirty or more banks, and so got a fund of $100,000 or more with which to discount bills.

In October, 1853, the present perfect Clearing House system was adopted, and has proved a great blessing to all the banks ever since. The entire exchanges of all the banks for the day, often amounting to over $100,000,000, are now made in six minutes, and the payment of balances consumes but a half-hour in the afternoon. It is the best proof of the admirable working of the system, that the exchanges of the banks for twenty-six years, amounting to over $200,000,000,000, have been made without an error, or loss of a single cent, and with a saving of ninety-seven per cent. of time and trouble over the old plan.

Our illustration, taken from "The Banks of New York" (published at Bankers' Magazine office), shows how the morning exchanges are made at New York.

Similar associations now exist in all the large cities— 24 are reported in the United States.   P.

MONEY ONE HUNDRED YEARS AGO.

Two hundred years ago, students at Harvard College paid their tuition with live-stock and provisions. The currency of the Pilgrims was the first issue of paper money in this country. During the war of Queen Anne a paper currency was established, known as Queen

Anne's war currency, which soon became worthless. In 1755, Virginia issued a paper currency, previous to which the clergy were paid in tobacco. In 1715, John Coleman established a bank in Massachusetts, with land for capital, and began the issue of loans. Other colonies followed, and the amount of loans by the colonies finally reached to millions, which the mother country paid off at reduced rates to save the credit of the colonies. In 1775 Congress issued paper currency to the amount of $300,000, to be redeemed in coin in three years. The Colonies or States also issued paper money, and soon the whole volume of State and National currency amounted to $12,000,000. This money was taken without much question at first, and those who refused it were stigmatized as unpatriotic ; but in the following year it began to decline, and in 1780 it was worth almost nothing. A barber-shop in Philadelphia was plastered all over with Continental money, and dogs were tarred, stuck over with the same shin-plasters, and let out to run the streets for the public amusement. To Robert Morris is due the salvation of the Revolutionary army. He lent his private fortune and credit to the government, and when all his money was gone and his credit had been liberally used, Washington said he must raise more money to carry out a war measure, the perfection of which only waited for the money. Morris therefore issued his own notes for $1,400,000. Washington gained the battle of Yorktown, and Cornwallis surrendered. Every one of these Morris notes were subsequently redeemed. In 1782, the Bank of North America was established at

Philadelphia, with a capital of $400,000. This was the first bank of the National Government.' The date of the first silver coinage was 1794, and of the first gold coinage 1794.

THE BANK OF ENGLAND, ITS WORKINGS AND REAL FUNCTIONS.

Few who read of the Bank of England have any real idea of the vastness of the operations of this greatest of the financial institutions of the world. London is a sort of clearing-house for all civilized nations, and around the Bank of England the commercial world may be said to revolve. The greatest amount of deposits in the whole of the New York banks has rarely, if ever, exceeded $250,000,000 ; those in this one London bank have reached more than half that sum, or $150,000,000. The New York banks' loans have varied sometimes $5,000,000 or $10,000,000 a week ; in one week, during a panic, the loans by the Bank of England rose over $50,000,000, and reached $155,000,000. or more than half the highest sum ever reached by the associated banks of New York. The greatness of the deposits is remarkable, especially as the bank pays no interest on them, and is surrounded by institutions that do. Another not less remarkable fact is that nearly forty per cent. of these deposits—at one time nearly $50,000,000—was placed in the bank by private bankers, despite the lack of interest. All these things show what is the real function of this vast establishment—security. So desirable is safety that the owners of $150,000,000 prefer to keep it in the bank's vaults without interest, rather than trust it elsewhere. The other function the bank has undertaken— to control the money-market—it has failed to achieve; but the safety it gives to funds has doubtless contributed much to lower the rate of interest in London. Great care and pains are taken to secure this safety. Every night twenty-five soldiers of the regular army are detailed to guard the bank; and, for the directors and managers, men of the highest character are selected. The movements of its deposits are watched with eagerness, and it has even been said that whenever they fall below $120,000,000, money is pretty sure to be scarce. The bank was 185 years old on the 27th of July, '79, having received a charter of incorporation at that date, and having been projected by William Paterson, a Scotchman. Constituted as a joint stock company, with a capital of £1,200,000, the whole sum was lent at interest to the government of William and Mary, then much embarrassed. At the outset it was a servant of the State, and has ever since continued such, more or less. The charter, granted at first for eleven years, has been from time to time renewed, the last renewal, subject to modification or revocation, having been in 1844. For a while the business was done in one room; now the bank occupies, as everybody knows, a large building in Threadneedle-street, and employs some 800 men. Nothing less than a £5 note is ever issued, and no note is issued a second time. The average amount of notes in circulation is £25,000,000.

EXPERIENCES AMONG THE FREED-MEN.

HIS "IN-TRUST."

Just before the failure of the Freedmen's Bank, a flashily dressed, cane-carrying colored citizen entered a branch bank, one morning, and said he desired "to acquire some information." Being requested to state his case, the brother proceeded: "I desiahs to know, sah, whethah, consequently, if this distinguished institootion should *fail*, would the *In-trust* go on juss the same untwill the 'positors is all settled therewith?" His pass book showing but forty-seven cents balance, his highness was informed that in his particular case no interest could be allowed. P.

A negro, overpaid $100 on a check, returned the money : a sure indication that the race can never be civilized. P.

DESIRABLE TERMS.

An ancient darkey leaned over a Clay street gate yesterday and called to the dusky proprietor of a cabin :

9   [193]

"See heah, Henry, isn't you 'bout ready to pay me dat two bits ?" "Haven't nuffin to pay wid," was the reply. "You borrowed dat money a whole year ago, Henry !" continued the old man. "Can't help dat—can't pay." "Henry, I believe you don't want to pay ; I believes you is dishonest, and I nebber ask for de money again ; I'll leave de Lord to collect it !" "Shoo !" exclaimed Henry, greatly interested all at once, "you hasn't enny more money to lend on dose terms, has ye ?" —*Free Press.*

NEGLECTED EDUCATION.

J. B. Smith, Boston's well-known colored caterer, presented a check at the bank the other day, and the teller asked him if he had any one to identify him. Mr. Smith, astonished, said : "Young man, don't you know me ?" The teller confessed that he did not. "Then," said Mr. Smith, "it is evident you have not moved in the first circles of society."

"INVESTIGATED."

One of our thrifty colored customers explained, as he drew a small amount from his savings account, that "I ain't triflin' this money for no foolishness, boss, but you see, me an' nine other fam'lies has jus' *investigated* ten dollars a head into a grocery store, an' so dat's what this yers for."

Another called recently, and desired a private interview with the cashier. He was walked back; when it appeared he desired to get a *divorce*, and he was "sure this was the right place, 'cos you is a fren' to the colored people, and as you is a notary republican, I's sure you can make it *illegiable*, so that all of 'em will be satisfied." He was sent on.

Another had recorded for his identification, that his birthday always came on the "third Monday in May."

· P.

CIVIL RIGHTS IN RALEIGH.

Ten years ago, this good one occurred in our State National Bank. As the portly president was walking out of the bank, he was confronted by a stalwart son of Afric's sunny clime, who, judging from the stream of water oozing from his garments, had been standing at the door in the rain for several hours.

"Spose yer name is Williams, is it?"

"My name, sir, is Mr. Williams."

"Dat's what I axed you—me'nt no harm; dis is de bank, de State bank, isn't it?"

"Yes, sir, this is the State National Bank."

"And de cibble rites is dun and pass'd, is it?"

"The civil rights bill is said to be the law of the land, sir."

"Dat's what I axed you, no harm meant; and ain't cullud pussons got as much rite to 'posit money here as de white folks?"

"They have the same privileges as white people in that particular, sir."

"Well den, just take dis pile ober dar and put it agin my name on de book." (Pulling from his side pocket about $300 in currency.)

Like a sensible man as he is, the president yielded to the majesty of the law, and took the " man and brother's" money on deposit.

Now, all this occurred on the crowded thoroughfare of Fayetteville street in open daylight. No police were called in, and no "nigger" killed. Who will say that we are not strictly loyal?

A FINANCIAL UNDERSTANDING.

We received, the other day, a call from an immaculately attired African citizen, artificially perfumed, and wearing yellow kids and a silk hat, who, after inquiring as to the state of our health, the weather, &c., struck an attitude, and this conversation ensued :

CITIZEN. (Twirling the rose in his button-hole.) Ah, I have called, sah, for the purpose, sah, of—ah—obtaining a sort of—ah—*financial understanding*, sah !

CASHIER. (Brusquely.) Well, what is it ?

CIT. Well, sah, the infohmation desiahed, sah, is about on this circumstance, sah. I had the honah, sah, some four weeks since, sah, to make a deposit in your distinguished institution, sah, and I neglected to ascertain—ah—the necessary remunerations as to your payments of —ah—interest.

CASH. Oh, yes. Interest is six per cent., paid July and January.

A FINANCIAL UNDERSTANDING.—*Page* 196.

Cᴛ. Precisely. So I inferred. May I trouble you to infohm me, sah, consequently, how the account is accumulating at present, sah ?

On examination of the ledger, cashier discovers that just four weeks previous, the man and brother had deposited *five dollars* as the nucleus of a savings account—and his fortune. His accumulations of interest (or in-*trust*, as our colored customers invariably term it) had reached the colossal figures of just *two and a half cents !*

This "financial understanding" was made in brief terms, and the individual withdrew, profoundly impressed with the deep depths of the great subject of finance.   P.

ELIMINATING HIS NOTE.

Said the pastor of the ——— Colored Church, who had a small note falling due, the other day, as he came in to fix it :

"Mr. Cashier, I wish to *eliminate* my note now due : on what terms can I do it ?"

Cashier replies, hardly grasping his idea : " We are always glad to have notes eliminated, and *cash* is about the best thing we know of to do it with."

But this wasn't his strong point. He desired to pay the "*in-trust*," and have a continuation, rather than an elimination, as we found out at last. But the average African-descended citizen will never outgrow his love of high-sounding talk.   P.

The Texas "man and brother" differeth not from the Virginia sort, as the genial cashier of the Houston Savings Bank goes on to illustrate :

HOUSTON, TEXAS, *Jan.* 10, 1879.

The love of hifalutin language, by the darkies of the Southern States, provokes many ludicrous incidents in the Queen's English.

Some time ago a freedman opened a small account at this bank. We gave him a pass-book, and in reply to usual inquiries from himself, explained the manner of keeping the money, and paying him "intrust," as he termed it. He was very anxious to caution us not to let anybody else draw his money but him, which we promised not to do !

"If anybody brings my book," quoth he, "and wants to draw the money, don't let him have it, till *I issue my knowledge to that refect !*"

After that we fainted dead away.

———————

COLORED SOCIETIES IN THE SOUTH.

The "late emancipated" down here in Dixie have a mania for organizing all sorts of societies and "*'stutions,*"- and then opening small bank accounts for the same. We find the following represented upon our books, the unique and highly appropriate names indicating some originality of idea, to say the least, and there are hundreds more—Wandering Pilgrims, Noble Sons of Israel, Rising Stars of Jerusalem, Enterprising Daughters of Galilee, Sons of Simeon, Female Israelites of Zion,

Corinthian Traveling Sons and Daughters of Colenia!
(Balance $1.24), Benevolent Daughters of Noah, Rising
Children of the Undergrowth ! (a juvenile organization),
Independent Rising Sons of Liberty, Union Stars, Sons
of Honor, Union Doves (these " Doves " being old men
of sixty or more brief summers), Humble Sons of God,
Enterprising Chartering Company No. 1., Sons and
Daughters of St. Paul (?), Oystering Association, and
the Wrestling Sons and Daughters of Jacob !—who, for
short, term themselves the " *Rasslin Jacobs*," and, finally,
The Messengers of Peace and Followers of Noah's Ark !

No matter how small the amount to deposit, it is invariably brought in by a committee of several persons,
who, if allowed, would consume an hour's time in per-
forming the duty, and it is the best minstrel show on
earth to see them do it.

EXTINCT.

The Finance Committee of a colored society connected with one of their large churches came in to bank
a few nickels with us, and while noting the particulars
in the signature book, instructed us to be mighty careful
not to mix their money with any other 'stution, as there
were four *ex*-tinct societies of de same title in dat church.
We endeavored to make the proper ex-tinction.

"ON CALL."

"I can't jess git frew my head how dose business

men can borrow money on call an' make it pay," Brother
Gardner was explaining at the market yesterday.   " De
odder day I borrowed two dollars of dat Mister Brown,
on Grove street, an' I was jess dat fool 'nuff to want to
show off a leetle, so I tole him I wanted to borrow dat two
dollar bill on call.   Well, what you s'pose happened ?"

" He didn't have any two dollars to lend !" called out
one of the whitewashers.

" You got de money and jumped de town !" put in a
second.

" Gemlen, I knows dis town, an' dis town knows me,"
stiffly replied Mr. Gardner.   "I believes my money is as
good as my word among the best business men in Detroit.   No, sir ; I tuk de money, went home, an' I hadn't
been in de house ten minutes when that Brown cum
along an' sung out :

" 'Brudder Gardner, I'ze calling over de fence for dat
two dollar bill !'

" Dere dat money was on call, an' dere he was calling
for it, an' I had to hand 'em ober.   When an old man
like me hez got his mind made up to have fried oysters
for breakfast, an' a finanshul smash like dat comes down
upon him, it jess makes de shivers go up'n down his
back widout regard to ceremony."

THE WRONG BOOK.

He was a disappointed African who presented a
blank pass-book at our counter, and called for $50.

When told that he hadn't the right sort of book, he was quite "set back," and asked, "Whah does you get the right book, sah?" He had seen lots of people drawing out money on similar books, and so had bought a blank book at the book-store, supposing he then had the true inwardness of the bank!

———————

A customer told us he had lived in Norfolk "ever since the vaccination of Suffolk" (meaning evacuation)

———————

At a "committee meeting" of the Freedman's Bank, a worthy brother remarked: "If I had the combined eloquence of the gem'len who has superseded me, I should try to answer his insinuendoes," &c., &c.

———————

OUR COLORED MESSENGER.

It is amusing to notice the wrath of the typical Southron, when one of the late emancipated assumes the business of white folks. Our bank is located in one of the reconstructed States, where colored labor is plentiful, and I had occasion, for a time, to employ as clerk and messenger a bright mulatto young man, who, besides being as smart as his average white neighbors, is of pleasing address, and (what is another damnable offense), a college graduate.

One of our retail merchants illustrated the popular sentiment, the other, day, rather more forcibly than usual. Meeting him on the street, he accosted me with scowling face : " Mr. Cashier, what do you mean, sending out *niggers* to present drafts to *me?* Can't your bank employ *white folks?*" I mildly suggested that as *we paid* our messengers, we should be allowed the privilege of selecting them ; and that while we were not bound to please him in the selection, we hoped, nevertheless, to employ none but *gentlemen,*—and asked if our runner had been guilty of any "impudence." "Oh, no, no," said he, shaking his fist in our face, in the most Christian (?) manner possible, " but it's just this ; if you ever send a d—n nigger to my store again with a draft, it'll not be accepted or paid, *and don't you forget it !*"

We intimated our willingness to employ a special messenger for his drafts if he would pay the bill, but if not, we had no concern as to his action, assuring him our notary would give the customary attention to all his dishonored paper ; which he did quite frequently thereafter, until the failure and closing-up of the high-toned and chivalric, but impecunious merchant.

STATISTICAL.

A BOOK much larger than this could easily be filled with interesting statistics, respecting the mission of the world's bankers ; but, as the greater part of these are regularly published in Bankers' Magazines and Financial Chronicles, of easy access, we only insert here a brief chapter, out of respect to the absorbing love for *facts* and *figures* and *precedents*, which the American people so universally exhibit.

"Nothing in the world is so false as *facts*,—except *figures*," quoth the cynical schoolmaster. Let us begin the chapter with the charmingly innocent letter of a Turkish Cadi to Mr. Layard, the Oriental traveler, in reply to his inquiries respecting the wealth and population of his own city :

"MY ILLUSTRIOUS FRIEND, AND JOY OF MY LIVER !

"The thing you ask of me is both difficult and useless. Although I have passed all my days in this place, I have neither counted the houses, nor have I inquired into the number of the inhabitants ; and as to what one person loads on his mules, and another stows away in the bottom of his ship, that is no business of mine. But, above all, as to the previous history of this city, God only knows the amount of dirt and confusion that the infidels may have eaten before the coming of the sword of Islam. It were unprofitable for us to inquire

into it. O my soul ! O my lamb ! Seek not after the
things which concern thee not. Thou camest unto us
and we welcomed thee : go in peace !

"Of a truth thou hast spoken many words; and
there is no harm done, for the speaker is one, and the
listener another. After the fashion of thy people, thou
hast wandered from one place to another, until thou art
happy and content in none. We (praise be to God)
were born here, and never desire to quit it. Is it possible, then, that the idea of a general intercourse between
mankind should make any impression on our under-
standings? God forbid !

"Listen, O my son ! There is no wisdom equal unto
the belief in God ! He created the world ; and shall we
liken ourselves unto him in seeking to penetrate into
the mysteries of his creation ? Shall we say—behold,
this star spinneth around that star, and this other
star with a tail goeth and cometh in so many years ?
Let it go ! He, from whose hand it came, will guide
and direct it.

"But thou wilt say unto me, Stand aside, O man, for I
am more learned than thou art, and have seen more things.
If thou thinkest that thou art in this respect better
than I am, thou art welcome. I praise God that I seek
not that which I require not. Thou art learned in the
things I care not for ; and as for that which thou hast
seen I defile it. Will much knowledge create thee a
double belly, or wilt thou seek paradise with thine eyes ?

"O my friend ! if thou wilt be happy, say there is no
God but God ! Do no evil, and thus wilt thou fear
neither man nor death ; for surely thine hour will come!

"The meek in spirit (El Fakir),

                              "IMAUM ALI ZADÈ."

Any readers who famish for more statistics than are here afforded, will find ample enjoyment and profit in that overflowing treasury of facts, "Spofford's American Almanac," for the current year, in which Mr. Spofford (the distinguished Librarian of Congress) presents, in most compact form, about all the facts and statistics for which even an American would be likely to inquire. (Am. News Co., N. Y., $1.50.)

NUMBER OF BANKS IN THE COUNTRY.

We find reported on January 1, 1879, the whole number of banking institutions in the United States, exclusive of brokers, whose name is *legion*, 6,085 banks, classified as follows ;

National Banks . . .	2,058
State Banks	874
Private Banks . . .	2,552
Savings Banks . . .	601
Total Banks . . .	6,085

SAVINGS BANK STATISTICS.

We compile from the published reports, the following interesting table, showing the present strength of Savings Banks, in those States where they are most popular.

STATISTICS OF UNITED STATES SAVINGS BANKS,

FROM REPORTS FOR THE YEAR 1878.

STATE.	NO. OF BANKS.	AMOUNT OF DEPOSITS.	TITLE OF LARGEST BANK AND AMOUNT OF ITS DEPOSITS.	
Maine..............	56	$25,708,472	Portland Savings Bank..............	$3,803,769
New Hampshire....	66	28,789,549	Manchester Savings Bank..........	2,984,123
Vermont...........	21	6,722,691	Burlington Savings Bank.......	1,395,516
Massachusetts......	168	244,596,614	New Bedford Inst. for Savings........	8,957,410
Rhode Island.......	37	48,103,119	Providence Inst. for Savings..........	8,203,326
Connecticut........	87	77,214,372	Hartford Society for Savings.........	7,841,581
New Jersey.........	35	16,353,275	Newark Savings Inst...............	13,687,075
California.........	26	70,984,764	Hibernian Savings and Loan Society....	15,283,080
New York City.....	24	164,536,153	Bowery Savings Bank..............	32,055,398
New York State, excl. of N. Y. City.	} 102 {	148,286,905	Brooklyn Savings Bank.............	15,235,451
Pennsylvania........		17,923,825	Philadelphia Saving Fund Society......	14,446,207
Maryland...........		19,739,206	Savings Bank of Baltimore..........	12,633,162

SEAMEN'S BANK FOR SAVINGS.
(74 *and* 76 *Wall street, New York City.*)

GROWTH OF SAVINGS BANKS IN NEW YORK STATE.

The marvelous growth of Savings Banks in this country is best illustrated by these figures from KEYES' HISTORY OF SAVINGS BANKS, showing their progress in the Empire State.

Year.	No. Banks.	No. Accounts.	No. Deposits.
1818	1	1,481	$148,195
1829	5	16,184	2,263,450
1839	12	34,716	4,794,613
1849	17	92,975	16,661,752
1859	64	273,697	58,178,160
1869	133	651,474	194,360,217
1874	158	872,498	303,935,649

Total Deposits for 55 years, . . $1,969,347,200
Total Amount withdrawn, . . . 1,665,411,551
_____
Due Depositors, . . . 303,935,649

Concerning this record of fifty-five years, Mr. Keyes says :

" No words of mine can add aught to the impressiveness of the record as there disclosed. It speaks for itself with an eloquence which it were foolish and vain for me to attempt to rival. And when we reflect that this record is but the mere exponent, sign, indication, of a history of social influences and human experiences that are unrecorded and undisclosed, hidden away in the secret chambers of human hearts, silently contributing to the happiness of millions of human lives, the power and vastness of this agency pass beyond the range of numerical computations, and reach the confines of the illimitable.

"This tabulated history is far less wonderful and thrilling than would be a revelation of the unwritten work accomplished through this agency. The frugality and thrift of which it has been the parent, the latent energies of labor which it has stimulated and brought into exercise, the foundations of future fortunes which have been laid through its instrumentality, the want, suffering, and despair that have been kept away from thousands of homes through its provident ministry, the guileless virtue which it has shielded from the temptations of poverty and hunger—if these could be spread before the eye in tangible, embodied form, though the record were then to close, the history of the last fifty years would be luminous with the light of these beneficent experiences, through all the coming ages."

HOW TO OPEN A LEDGER ALPHABETICALLY.

To assist book-keepers, who are often at a loss how to proceed in opening a new Ledger alphabetically, we give the following Table of Apportionment for a 1,200 page Ledger, for which credit "*Gould's Universal Index.*"

	a,	e,	i,	o,	u,	y,
A.	1	16	32	52	64	68
B.	72	96	116	124	144	156
C.	160	208	220	232	280	292
D.	296	308	320	328	336	344
E.	348	368	384	396	400	400
F.	404	412	424	436	456	456
G.	460	472	480	488	492	492
H.	496	508	516	524	536	540
I.	544	548	556	560	560	560
J.	564	568	568	572	580	580
K.	584	588	596	600	600	600
L.	604	612	620	628	636	636
M.	640	672	676	684	700	704
N.	708	712	720	728	736	736
O.	740	744	752	756	756	756
P.	760	788	808	824	836	844
R.	848	856	868	876	896	900
S.	904	924	956	996	1016	1016
T.	1020	1036	1044	1056	1084	1092
U.	1096	1100	1104	1104	1104	1104
V.	1108	1120	1120	1124	1124	1124
W.	1128	1140	1152	1172	1180	1180
X.	1184	1184	1184	1184	1184	1184
Y.	1184	1184	1188	1188	1188	1188
Z.	1192 to	1196	Q.	1196	to	1200

OUR PAPER CURRENCY.

The amount of paper currency in circulation in the United States, on June 30, 1878, was as follows :

Legal Tenders	$346,681,016
National Currency	324,514,284
State Bank Notes	426,504
Demand Notes	62,297
One and two-year Notes of 1863	90,485
Compound Interest Notes	274,920
Fractional Currency	16,547,769
Total	$688,597,275

VALUABLE UNITED STATES COINS.

Many persons may not be aware that the following U. S. coins, on account of their scarcity, command a considerable premium, varying according to their state of preservation. Messrs. Scott & Co., 146 Fulton street, N. Y., will pay from 25 to 500 per cent. over the face value, for any contained in the following list :

Dollars, 1794, 1804, 1838, 1839, 1851, 1852.

Half dollars, 1794, 1796, 1797, 1815.

Quarter dollars, 1823, 1827.

Dimes, 1796, 1797, 1798, 1800, 1801, 1802, 1803, 1804, 1809, 1811, 1822, 1824.

Half dimes, 1794, 1795, 1796, 1797, 1800, 1801, 1802, 1803, 1805.

Copper cents, 1793, 1796, 1799, 1804, 1806, 1809, 1811, 1813.

Nickel cent, 1856.

Half cents, 1793, 1796, 1802, 1811.

INTEREST LAWS IN FORCE IN 1878.

[FROM BANKERS' ALMANAC.]

State.	Rate per cent.		Penalty of Usury.
	Legal.	Special.	
1 Alabama.....	8	—	Loss of interest.
2 Arizona......	10	§	None.
3 Arkansas......	6	10	Forfeiture of principal and interest.
4 California....	10	§	None.
5 Colorado.....	10	§	None.
6 Connecticut...	6	6	None.
7 Dakota.......	7	12	Forfeiture of contract.
8 Delaware.....	6	6	Forfeiture of contract.
9 Dist. of Col...	6	10	Forfeiture of all interest
10 Florida.......	8	§	None.
11 Georgia......	7	12	Forfeiture of all interest.
12 Idaho *10		24	$100, or imprisonment 6 months, or both.
13 Illinois.......	6	10	Forfeiture of all the interest.
14 Indiana	6	10	Forfeiture of interest over 10 per cent.
15 Iowa.........	6	10	Forfeiture of interest and costs.
16 Kansas.......	7	12	Forfeiture of excess over 12 per cent.
17 Kentucky	6	6	Forfeiture of excess of interest.
18 Louisiana....	5	8	Forfeiture of interest.
19 Maine	6	§	None.
20 Maryland	6	6	Forfeiture of excess.
21 Massachusetts	6	§	None. (Six per cent. on judgments.)

* Usurers liable to arrest for misdemeanor.
† Rate on judgments unless otherwise expressed.
‡ On railroad bonds only.   § No limit.
| No corporation can plead usury.

Rate per cent.

State.	Legal.	Special.	Penalty of Usury.
22 Michigan.....	7	10	Forfeiture of excess.
23 Minnesota....	7	12	Forfeiture of contract if more than 12 per cent. is charged.
24 Mississippi...	6	§	Forfeiture of interest over 10 per cent.
25 Missouri......	6	10	Forfeiture of all interest.
26 Montana.....	10	§	None.
27 Nebraska.....	10	12	Forfeiture of all interest, and costs.
28 Nevada......	10	§	None.
29 N. Hampshire	6	6	Forfeiture of three times the interest received.
30 New Jersey...	6	6	Forfeiture of all interest and costs.
31 New Mexico.	6	§	None.
32 New York....	*7	7	Forfeiture of contract ; $1000 fine ; 6 months imprisonment.
33 N. Carolina..	6	8	Forfeiture of double amount of interest.
34 Ohio.........	6	8	Forfeiture of excess.
35 Oregon	10	12	Forfeiture of interest, principal and costs.
36 Pennsylvania.	6	6	Forfeiture of excess. *Act May* 28, 1858.
37 Rhode Island.	†6	§	Forfeiture, unless a greater rate is contracted.
38 South Carolina	7	7	Forfeiture of all the interest.
39 Tennessee....	6	6	Forfeiture of excess over 6 per cent.
40 Texas........	8	12	Forfeiture of all interest.
41 Utah.........	10	§	None.
42 Vermont.....	6	‡7	Forfeiture of excess.
43 Virginia......	6	ǀ	Forfeiture of interest.
44 Washington T.	10	§	None.
45 West Virginia.	6	6	Forfeiture of excess.
46 Wisconsin....	7	10	Forfeiture of all the interest.
47 Wyoming	10	§	None.

* Usurers liable to arrest for misdemeanor.
† Rate on judgments unless otherwise expressed.
‡ On railroad bonds only.   § No limit.
ǀ No corporation can plead usury.

VALUE OF "GRAY-BACKS" IN THE GOOD OLD NORTH STATE.

ACT OF THE LEGISLATURE OF NORTH CAROLINA IN 1865.

Be it enacted by the General Assembly of the State of North Carolina, that the following scale of depreciation be, and the same is hereby adopted and established as the measure of value of one gold dollar in Confederate currency for each month (and the fractional parts of the month of December, 1864), from the 1st day of November, 1861, to the 1st day of May, 1865, to wit :

MONTHS.	1861.	1862.	1863.	1864.	1865.
January...................	..	1 20	3 00	21 00	50 00
February..................	..	1 30	3 00	21 00	50 00
March	..	1 50	4 00	23 00	60 00
April.....................	..	1 50	5 00	20 00	100 00
May	..	1 50	5 50	19 00	
June......................	..	1 50	6 50	18 00	
July......................	..	1 50	9 00	21 00	
August....................	..	1 50	14 00	23 00	
September.................	..	2 00	14 00	25 00	
October...................	..	2 00	14 00	26 00	
November.................	1 10	2 50	15 00	30 00	
December.................	1 15	2 50	20 00		
December 1st to 10th, in-clusive	....	....	....	35 00	
December 11th to 20th, in-clusive	....	....	....	42 00	
December 21st to 31st, in-clusive	....	....	....	149 00	

HOW MUCH IS A BILLION?

"A billion is a million times a million. Can you count it? Perhaps you can count 160 or 170 in a minute : nay, suppose you can count even 200 in a minute ; then in one hour you could count 12,000, if you were not interrupted. Well, 12,000 an hour would be 288,000 a day : and a year, or 365 days, would produce 105,120,000 !

"But this wouldn't allow you a single moment for sleep, nor for any other business whatever. Well, now suppose that Adam, at the beginning of his existence, had begun to count, had continued to count, and was counting still ; he would not even now, according to the usual supposed age of our globe, have counted near enough. For, to count a billion, he would require 8,512 years, 34 days, 5 hours, and 20 minutes, according to the above reckoning. But suppose we were to allow the poor counter twelve hours daily for rest, eating, and sleeping, he would need 19,024 years, 68 days, 10 hours, and 40 minutes to count a billion !"

Just remember this, when some generous friend hands you over a present of a billion, and asks you to "look it over, and see if the amount is correct !"

BANK FOR SAVINGS.

(67 *Bleecker street, New York City.*)

Page 215.

NEW YORK SAVINGS BANKS.
[CONTRIBUTED.]

The rise and progress of Savings Banks in the Empire State furnishes a fitting example of the beneficent results wrought out through the agency of all such institutions.

It is a noticeable fact that a movement to organize a Savings Bank was instituted about the same time in Philadelphia, New York and Boston. This was in the latter part of the year 1816. In New York, an organization was effected November 29, in that year, but it did not go into operation until nearly three years later. The prevalence of poverty in those days was the prime cause which rendered a Savings Bank necessary. The gentlemen who took the initiative in the work, meeting with much opposition in the Legislature, the original bill to incorporate the bank being defeated, they formed themselves into a "Society for the Prevention of Pauperism," and from that stand-point advocated the favorable influences of Savings Banks in arresting the progress of pauperism and crime.

The pioneer institution, known as the "Bank for Savings in the City of New York," was incorporated March 26, 1819, and in the following July a place was opened for receiving deposits. The spirit manifested in the State Legislature which retarded this enterprise for a time, could not now keep it back. The savings bank idea had sprung from master minds; the character of those who formulated the system gave it the impress of beneficence.

But the early growth of the system was not rapid. The Bank for Savings was four years in accumulating its first million of deposits. Now it receives from five to six millions annually, has on deposit over $27,000,000, belonging to over eighty thousand persons, and has paid out in interest to depositors, from organization to and including the dividend of January, 1879, the sum of $24,533,996!

Covering the first two decades of savings bank history in the State of New York, the banks organized during that period exhibit a similar slow but sure progress. In 1840, there were but twelve banks for savings in the State, with aggregate deposits of $5,431,966. Now there are one hundred and thirty-two banks, with deposits of about $300,000,000. The following table shows the growth of these institutions as shown by their deposits from 1850 to 1879:

1850,	. . . .	$20,832,972
1855,	. . . .	26,012,713
1860,	. . . .	67,440,397
1865,	. . . .	115,472,566
1870,	. . . .	230,749,408
1875,	. . . .	319,260,202
1876,	. . . .	316,677,285
1877,	. . . .	312,823,058
1878,	. . . .	299,074,639

The aggregate surplus January 1, 1879, was $34,553,262, and the depositors numbered 810,017, showing an average of $369 of deposits, and a guarantee surplus of over $42 to each depositor, equal to a safety fund averaging 11 38-100 per cent.

From the time the system was founded in New York (1819) down to January 1, 1879, a period of sixty years,

CITIZENS' SAVINGS BANK.

(S. W. corner of Bowery and Canal street, New York City.)

the amount deposited foots up the enormous sum of $2,464,841,677, nearly twenty-five hundred million dollars! The interest paid to depositors in the same time amounts to $216,075,773 !!

Note.—The following are some noteworthy facts in the history of savings banks in the State of New York :

1. The first thirty-five years were entirely free from failures. Fifty years passed and the loss to depositors was an inconsiderable sum. In 1871, two failures, both banks under "Ring" rule. In 1872-3, three failures.

WILLIAMSBURGH SAVINGS BANK.
(149 *Broadway, Brooklyn, E. D., L. I.*)

2. In 1875, a General Savings Bank Law was passed, conforming the banks to equal rights, liabilities and powers. Before that time each institution was operated under its own charter.

3. From 1875 to 1879, twenty-four failures. Amount

due depositors in all the failed banks, about $15,000,000 ; of this amount a trifle over one-half has been returned to depositors—the balance goes to the receivers, lawyers, "assistant wreckers," referees, &c.

4. In the summer of 1877, Mr. H. L. Lamb, the Bank Superintendent's deputy or assistant, "*fell on the mantle* of his deposed superior" (as *Rhodes' Journal of Banking* puts it), and since then he has been in charge of the department. Thus far his record cannot be described as enviable. In order to gratify his desire to make a show of extraordinary vigilance, many of his acts have been calculated to impair public confidence and bring the institutions and their management into disfavor. Under the New York law extraordinary powers are given to the Bank Superintendent, and in the hands of an incapable or unscrupulous man, the office may be subserved to personal and selfish aims.

GENERAL VIEW OF SAVINGS BANKS IN THE UNITED STATES.

[WRITTEN FOR THE BANKERS' SCRAP-BOOK.]

The Savings Banks of the United States are institutions for safely investing small sums saved from the wages of labor, and paying interest on the same, and returning the principal at short notice. The first savings bank in the country was started in Philadelphia in 1816. Others went into operation in New York, Boston, Baltimore, and many New England towns, during the three following years.

In a majority of the States the savings banks are

operated under the regulations of general law; in others the courts have jurisdiction over them, while in some localities the banks of this class are simply private concerns with the sign "Savings Bank" over their doors. The latter are growing less in number each year.

Another marked difference in savings banks is their mode of organization : those in the New England States, New York and New Jersey are all organized as mutual or non-capital institutions. A limited number in Pennsylvania, Ohio, Indiana and Minnesota are also conducted on this plan. In the other States where savings banks are in operation, they are organized on the basis of a capital stock, which is paid in (or subscribed and part paid) by the corporators, as an additional guarantee to the depositors. The banks without capital are sometimes called "provident institutions," and are described in the United States Revised Statutes (section 3408) as "having no capital stock and doing no other business than receiving deposits, to be loaned or invested for the sole benefit of the parties making such deposits, without profit or compensation to the association company."

The system of savings banks in the United States would be greatly strengthened if the banks in the various States were more nearly uniform in their powers, rights and liabilities. The absence of State regulation, or of any authoritative supervision whatever, in some localities, prevents any full knowledge of their affairs. This condition frequently breeds loss of confidence by depositors,

consequent disaster follows, and the entire system
suffers.

The following table shows the aggregate resources of
savings banks in the United States, on or about the first
of January of the years named :

1875,	.	.	.	.	$896,197,454
1876,	.	.	.	.	951,353,544
1877,	.	.	.	.	922,794,562
1878,	.	.	.	.	941,447,150

The number of savings banks is tabulated in the report of the Comptroller of the Currency, December 2,
1878, as follows :

New England States	.	.	.	442
Middle States	.	.	.	193
Southern States	.	.	.	7
Western States and Territories	.	49
Total in United States	.	.	691

This is doubtless the number of savings banks which
report either to State departments or to the United
States Internal Revenue Department, for the purposes of
taxation. The actual number doing business under the
title "Savings Bank," amounts to over one thousand.

It may be safely stated from the returns which do
exist, that the amount of deposits in savings banks
throughout the United States reaches, if it does not exceed, $1,000,000,000 (one thousand millions), held by about
2,800,000 depositors, while the amount of annual interest,
or dividends, paid by savings banks, exceeds $45,000,000.

The only extended and comprehensive account of these institutions may be found in "Keyes' History of Savings Banks in the United States." In referring to the growth of savings banks in this country, the author says : " This growth, from the best data we are able to gather, was, during the ten years preceding the war, from about $43,300,000, to nearly $150,000,000, or nearly two hundred and fifty per cent.; probably, if we could obtain exact data, it would be quite equal to that. The increase from 1840 to 1850, being from about $14,000,000 to $43,000,000, was a smaller per cent. than the above, but was still a marked and wonderful development." After referring to a comprehensive table in the work above referred to, showing the growth and progress of savings banks in the United States from 1820 down to the present, the author says : " Of course this table, grand and wonderful as is the record which it presents, falls far short of revealing the whole work accomplished by savings banks since their introduction into this country. This can only be estimated in the most general way, with many elements for a correct calculation wanting. I should make a rough estimate in this way about as follows : Whole number of accounts opened, 8,700,000 ; amount deposited, $4,750,000,000 ; interest credited, $300,000,000."

The illustrations on the preceding pages show the bank buildings of three well-known savings banks in the city of New York, and one in Brooklyn, E. D. (Williamsburgh).

POST OFFICE SAVINGS BANKS IN CANADA.

A statement showing business done at the Post Office Savings Banks from 1st April, 1868, to 30th June, 1879, has been printed. Since the last day of June interest has been calculated, and balance struck of the accounts of 27,445 depositors. There are in the Dominion 297 post offices which receive deposits. The number of depositors is 27,445, and the amount standing to their credit on June 30th was $2,925,290.80, or nearly three million dollars. Interest is allowed at the rate of four per cent., except on $179,900, which draws five per cent., and it is stated that no new deposits to draw five per cent. have been accepted since 1871. The following figures show the total amounts due depositors on 30th of June in each year named, that for 1868 being accumulation of three months' business, only the beginning having been made on the first of April of that year :

1868	$130,688	1872	$2,144,600	1876	$2,432,852
1869	153,614	1873	2,508,651	1877	2,375,537
1870	939,938	1874	2,692,865	1878	2,498,400
1871	1,396,559	1875	2,525,390	1879	2,925,290

—*Monetary Times, Toronto.*

ORIGIN OF BANKS.

The name "bank" is derived from *banco,* a bench erected in the market-place for the exchange of money.

The first was established in Italy, 808, by the Lombard Jews, of whom some settled in Lombard street, London, where many bankers still reside. The Mint in the Tower of London was anciently the depository for merchants' cash, until Charles I. laid his hands upon the money and destroyed the credit of the Mint, in 1640. The traders were thus driven to some other place of security for their gold, which, when kept at home, their apprentices frequently absconded with to the army. In 1645, therefore, they consented to lodge it with the goldsmiths in Lombard street, who were provided with strong chests for their own valuable wares ; this became the origin of banking in England.

—*Haydn's Dictionary of Dates.*

SUBSTITUTE FOR MONEY.

The principal market in Guernsey was built without money. The governor issued four thousand market notes, and with these paid the workmen who built it. These notes circulated through the island, until the market was built and occupied ; and when the rents came in, these notes were received in payment of the rents, and were canceled. In the course of a few years, the notes, being all paid in, were publicly burned in the market.

The Water Works, Upper Canada, were constructed by a similar use.

TRAGICAL.

TRAGICAL RESULT OF LOSING BANK NOTES.

ONE of the most tragical events in the business world took place awhile ago in St. Petersburg. The agent of a banker, who had been to the bank to receive the value of fifteen thousand silver roubles, lost the package of bank notes on his return. The money was picked up by a clerk, who, instead of giving the funds at once to the owner, followed the agent to his destination, and in this way ascertained his name. The clerk then returned home, hesitating in his own mind how he should act. When he arrived there, a violent quarrel took place between him and his wife, the latter wishing to keep the money. The clerk, however, on the following day, went to the house of the owner to deliver the money, but the banker would not receive it, saying his agent had committed suicide in the night, on account of the loss. Overcome with remorse, the clerk returned home, where he found that, during his absence, his wife had hanged herself from vexation at not having kept the money. He immediately cut down the body, and hung himself with the same rope.

10*   [225]

JOHN W. BARRON,

MURDERED AT HIS POST.—"FAITHFUL UNTO DEATH."

Through the kindness of the publishers of RHODES' JOURNAL, whose issue of April, 1879, contained a full account of the death of the Hero Cashier, *John W. Barron*, of Dexter, Maine, we insert his portrait, and an abridgment of the article there published.

The sublime heroism of this quiet, unassuming man, who surrendered his life rather than his trust, has been the topic of the New England press for months, and his name will deservedly pass into history.

On Washington's Birthday, 1878, Mr. Barron improved the holiday by writing at the bank. Failing to come home at the usual hour, his wife became anxious, and persuaded a neighbor to call at the bank to see if all was right. The result is familiar to all who read the papers. The neighbor found the cashier of the National Bank, and with him entered the building which his own and Mr. Barron's Savings Bank occupied. Both banks use a common vault for their safes, situated between their respective rooms, as shown in following diagram :

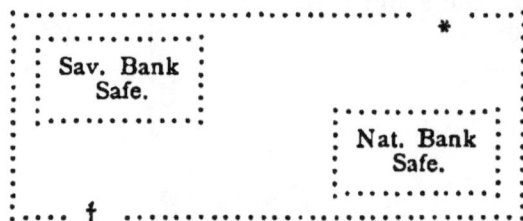

* Door from Savings Bank into vault.
† Door from National Bank into vault.

Faithfully Yours
J. W. Barron

CASHIER JOHN W. BARRON. MURDERED AT DEXTER, MAINE, 1878.—*Page* 226.

On opening the door of the vault used by the
National Bank, sounds of distress were heard from the
other side; but as the door of the Savings Bank safe was
open, and fastened open, thus blocking the space between the safes, they could not well reach the sufferer.
The door of the Savings Bank was then forced open,
when it was found that the vault door on this side was
closed and locked!

The men then tried again from the National Bank
side, and by great effort forced their way between the
safes and over the safe door, when, by the light of a
lantern, Mr. Barron was discovered in a most pitiable
condition. He lay in a distorted position, gagged, with
hands tightly fastened behind him by a pair of French
hand-cuffs, and had evidently been knocked senseless,
and lying there for more than two hours. An alarm was
given, other assistance came, and Mr. Barron's body was
got through the narrow space between the safes, and
into the National Bank office, where the manacles were
cut from his wrists, and medical aid summoned. Here
he lay, surrounded by physicians and kind friends, rallying but little from their kind ministrations until his death
at six next morning—his agonized wife remaining by
his bedside to the last.

The following notice, in an extra *Gazette*, shows the
feeling about this murder in Dexter :

"As will be seen by the account which we publish in
this extra edition of the *Gazette*, a terrible event has occurred in our town. One of the banking houses here

has been entered by burglars and robbed; and in trying to accomplish their designs the guilty wretches have murdered the treasurer, Mr. J. W. Barron, a gentleman who has grown up here among the people of Dexter, who is known to all, and known only to be respected and beloved. We doubt if there is a man in the whole State of Maine who has been engaged in one way and another with so many different people, and in such important positions, who has more thoroughly succeeded in keeping the good-will of all. He was such a man as Dexter, or any other town lucky enough to have him for a citizen, could ill afford to lose, even in the natural course of events. But when such a one is *murdered* because he stands in the way of a gang of cut-throats who are after money, we cannot even contemplate the idea without the most passionate feeling; and when we say this, we but reflect the heartfelt sentiment of every citizen of this community. We have never been an advocate of the Lynch law—we don't believe in it now, and should certainly oppose its execution by every means in our power—yet we but state what is a fact when we say that, in the present mood of this community, if Mr. Barron's murderer should be discovered, and could be reached by the people, his life would not be worth a farthing."

The money loss to the bank was trifling, the bank examiner reporting it as $628.82.

Some months after the murder, the public were astonished by a report from the officers of the bank that

Mr. Barron was not murdered at all, but had committed suicide to conceal his robbery of the bank. They claimed to have had a "thorough" examination, which brought out this, and their detective, one Dearborn, showed how it was quite possible for Mr. Barron to have locked himself into the vault, and arranged everything just as found when he was discovered. But, considering the fact that Mr. Barron was a quiet, village-bred citizen, unfamiliar with practical crime, that he showed no nervousness to his family on the fatal day, that his own pocket-book, containing about $500, has not been seen since his death, and that no irregularities, conflicting with the theory of his innocence, have yet come to light, the officers of the bank have found the public quite unwilling to believe their extraordinary statements. The circumstances of his death utterly preclude all idea of suicide, and this outrageous attack upon his memory seems, to all candid minds, a more cruel and damnable murder than that by which he lost his life.

On February 22, 1879, the anniversary of his death, a deeply-interesting memorial service was held at the Congregational Church in Dexter, at which a large audience was present. The church was appropriately draped, and adorned with floral designs. Back of, and above the platform, was placed a picture of Mr. Barron, against a background of black drapery, and over the platform was the motto, in evergreen, "FAITHFUL UNTO DEATH." Several clergymen took part in the exercises, Rev. J. S. Sewell, D.D., of the Bangor Theological Seminary, delivering a lengthy address upon the life, character, and death of Mr. Barron, all of which convinced him of the falseness of the theory of suicide, and strengthened him in the belief that Mr. Barron was indeed " Faithful unto death."

DISHONOR, BUT NOT DEATH.

From the middle of the Keystone State comes a cashier with this affidavit:

A certain M. D., having a drug store in our town, and having some notes maturing to several Philadelphia houses, and no money to meet them, and whose standing, financially, was considerably below par, believing his credit would be ruined entirely if his notes went to protest, and having been refused by several men whose indorsement he had solicited, came into our bank, and in a very excited manner informed me he had purchased a revolver, and was about to go home, make his will, and shoot himself. Brandishing the murderous weapon, he exhorted me not to mention it until all was over, but he had fully resolved, and should proceed at once to blow his brains out.

Recommending him to our bank's attorney as a suitable person to draw up his testamentary document, I bade him farewell, and he retired. To my surprise he actually visited the attorney, and had the will drawn and executed in due and ancient form. Whereupon my humanity overcame my good sense, and thinking it was a pity to let the poor man destroy himself, I called on him, and most earnestly reasoned the case over with him ; so effectually, too, that he relented, and didn't shoot. But he subsequently acted the fool so abominably, that I devoutly wished I had allowed the tragedy to proceed. When another customer of this bank desires to suicide, the cashier will be the last man to interpose any objection.

———◆———

STOCK GAMBLING SUICIDES.

The San Francisco *Chronicle* publishes, under the sign of a skull and cross-bones, and in a heavy black border, the names of sixty-five citizens of the town, who have committed suicide since 1874, on account of losses suffered in stock speculations. This is held up as a frightful argument against the existence of the · San Francisco Stock Board.

———◆———

DISCOUNTING A LEGACY.

It is related of TAYLOR, an eminent stock jobber in London, and who died worth half a million, that he was so penurious as to scarcely allow himself the necessaries of life. On his death-bed the officers of the parish waited upon him at his request, and found the old man on a wretched bed in a garret, dining on a thin slice of bacon and a potato, of which he asked them to partake. One of them accepting, the miser desired the cook to broil him another ; but, finding the larder totally empty,

Taylor rebuked her harshly for not having it well supplied with a *quarter of a pound* to cut out in slices for company. He then informed the overseers of the poor that he had left, by his will, one thousand pounds sterling for their relief, and eagerly inquired if they would not allow him *discount for prompt payment!* This being assented to, apparently much delighted, he immediately gave them a check for nine hundred and fifty pounds, and soon after breathed his last.

--------◆--------

THE BARRON MEMORIAL CHURCH.

The Congregational Church at Dexter, Maine, built in memory of the martyr cashier, Barron, is now nearly completed. It has been largely paid for by outside effort, among banks and bankers. Over $3,000 has been already raised, and about $800 more is needed. In view of the fact that the church edifice is a memorial to the murdered bank cashier, who was for years a deacon in this church, it would be a graceful and eminently proper thing if eight hundred cashiers about the country would, as soon as these lines are read, remit ONE DOLLAR EACH to Rev. J. S. Richards (Pastor of the church), Dexter, Me. A brick in this church is excellent property for a bank to own. How many will respond?

PERCY.

--------◆--------

A LECTURE ON FINANCE.

JOSH BILLINGS MAKES A FEW REMARKS.—*Page* 233.

JOSH BILLINGS.

BELIEVING our Scrap-Book would be incomplete without some clippings from the wisdom of this eminent financier and philosopher, we begged him to contribute, or allow us to embezzle some of his ideas, to which he promptly responded as follows :

March 26, 1879.
NEW YORK.

I dwell in New York.
I cannot,
My Dear Sir, furnish you with what you ask for, but you may *reach out* and *take* any*thing of mine* that is on the wing, for the especial purpose you ask for.
May your venture have Luck
is the prayer
of JOSH BILLINGS.

[As a P. S. he inclosed this financial chromo.]
[SEE PAGE 236.]

Josh Billings. and the Bull.

Never take the Bull bi the horns Yung Man, but take him bi the tale. Then yu kan let go when yu want to.—Yure warm friend. Josh Billings

APHORISMS, PRECEPTS, &c.

I hav finally cum to the konklushun that the best epitaff enny man kan hav, for all praktikall purposes, is a good bank ackount.

If yu undertake to hire a man to be honest, yu will hav to raize hiz wages every morning, and watch him dredphull cluss besides.

If yu want to find out the utter weakness ov munny, just try to hire a dubble tooth to stop akeing.

The devil is a very cunning phellow, but the blunders he makes allwuss eats up the proffitts in hiz bizzness.

This iz my plan—to beleave all things that i hear, but to put mi faith and munny in but few.

Dear Hank,—When you strike ile pull out yure auger at onst, and begin to barrell the ile; menny a man haz kept on until he bored klean thru, and sum other phellow kaught the grease at the bottom.

There may be sutch a thing as a man who haz stole once, and then quit, but i hav not the honor ov hiz acquaintance.

Mankind luv to be cheated, but they want to have it dun bi an artist.

It aint safe to endorse ennybody; we kant even tell ourselfs what kind ov a man we shall be on the 25th day of next june.

What a man gits for nothing, he iz very apt to value at just about what it kost.

There is a multitude of folks who mean well enuff, but how like the devel tha act.

If I was asked, "what is the chief end of man now a daze," I should immegiately repli, "ten per cent."

It aint often that a man's reputashun outlasts his munny.

It is dredful easy tew be a phool—a man kan be one and not know it.

Munny is like promises, easier maid than kept.

The fules in this wurld make about as much trubble as the wicked du.

I never argy agin a sucksess, when i see a rattlesnaixs

hed sticking out ov a whole, i bear off to the left, and say to myself—that whole belongs to that snaix.

I hav notised that all men are honist when well watched.

I say to 2 thirds ov the ritch people in this world — make the most ov yure money, for it makes the most ov yu = Happy Thought = Josh Billings

I luv a phool ; what little I kno I hav larnt by hanging around them.

He who suspekts everyboddy, should be watched by everyboddy.

A good karakter is allwuss gained bi inches, but iz often lost in one chunk.

Mi experience in life thus far haz been, that 7 won't go into 5, and hav mutch of ennything left over.

Lerning pays a better interest than munny duz, besides the principal never gits lost.

Don't change yure bait, mi boy, if you are ketching fish with angle worms—stik to the worms.

Don't never trust a man at the rate ov 50 cents on a dollar,—if you kant konfide in him at par, let him slide.

Young man, mark yure goose up hi : two-thirds ov the world hav no other idea of value, only by the price that iz put onto things.

The fust 3 notes i endorsed i had to pay, and i hope it will be jiss so with the next 3.

Tew enjoy a good reputashun, give publickly, and steal privately.

Tew remove grease from a man's karakter, let him strike sum sudden ile.

When i git thoroughly ritch, the fust thing i intend to dew iz tew bekum respektabel.

Better leave yure children virtew than money,—but this is a sekret known only to a few.

The time tew be karefullest iz when we hav a hand full ov trumps.

I hav allwus notised one thing, when a man gits in a tite spot, he don't never call on hiz friend the Devil tew help him out.

Prosperity makes phools, and adversity cures them.

I don't kno ov ennything more remorseless, on the face of the earth, than 7 per cent. interest.

A kicking cow never lets drive until just as the pail gets phull—it is jiss so with sum men's blunders.

The man who haint got an enemy iz really poor.

I never question a suckcess enny more than I do the right ov a bull dog to tie in hiz own gateway; no I dont, Josh Billings.

Thare iz two kind ov men that i don't kare to meet when i am in a grate hurry; men that i owe, and men that want to owe me.

Total depravity iz a hard thing for me to believe, but i must say, that i often meet cases that wouldn't pay more than 5 per cent. for rektifying.

The highest rate ov interest that we pay iz for

I thank the Lord that thare iz one thing in this world that money kant buy, and that iz — the wag ov a dogs-tail.=
Yure unkle, Josh Billings

borrowed trouble. Things that are alwus a-going tew happen, never do happen.

Blessed iz he who can pocket abuse, and feel that it iz no disgrace tew be bit bi a dog.

Money well spent iz well invested.

Take all the phools and good luk out ov this world, and it would bother the rest ov us tew git a living.

Yung man, dont be afrade to blo yure own horn, but dont blo it in front ov the proeeshun, go to the rear and do it. Yure uncle, Josh Billings.

A phool's money iz like hiz branes—very oneazy.

Next tew the man who iz worth a millyun, in point ov wealth. iz the man who don't kare a kuss for it.

One ov the handyest things a man kan do, is to giv hiz note for 90 daze.

Real good lies are gitting skarse.

Diogoneze hunted in the da time for an honest man, with a lantern ; if he had lived in theze times, he would hav needed the hed lite ov a lokomotiff.

The world iz bankrupt in morals, and if kind heaven won't settle with us for 10 cents on the dollar, the devil will git the whole thing bi foreclosure.

The man who *forgives,* and don't *forgit,* compounds for 50 cents on the dollar.

Whenever you cum akrost a man who distrusts everyboddy, you hav found one whom it is safe for everyboddy to distrust.

If you would eskape envy, abuse, and taxes, you must liv in a deep well, and only cum out in the nite time.

If you hav enny doubt about the propriety ov a thing, you may be pretty certain that the doubt is right.

Thare are folks who kant bear to do ennything unless thare iz a commishun in it ; if they subskribe a thousand dollars for bilding a church, they want 10 per cent. off for cash.

The man who haint never bin cheated, don't kno so mutch az he will sum day, before long perhaps.

THE MIZER.

The mizer digs hiz heart out hollow to stow away hiz munny in. He akumulates bi littles, and never opens hiz harte, only on a krak, to let another shilling in.

An old mizer iz a sad sight enuff, but next to an ideot, a young mizer iz the most revolting thing on earth. Mizers enjoy what they don't use, looze what they save, and die possessed ov the only treasure that iz ov no use to them. The most terrible sarkasm iz a mizer's phuneral, the heir often makes it gorgeous, and expensiv, and then pitches hedlong into the pile the old phool haz left.

Josh Billings, and the Yung Man.

Yung Man, dont kry for spilt milk, but pik up yure pail, and milking stool, and go for the next Cow.= Yures affekshionately, Josh Billings.

I don't take enny phoolish chances, if i waz called upon to mourn over a ded mule, i should stand in front ov him, and do mi weeping =
J. Billings Esq

The biggest phool in this world hazn't been born yet.

I think now if I had all the money that iz due me i would invest it in a saw mill, —— and let her rip.

Mankind love misterys; a hole in the ground excites more wonder than a star up in heaven.

Fools are the whet stuns ov society.

Thare iz nothing in this world that a man pays so hi a price for, and gits so little ov hiz munny back, as he duz for Repentance.

The miser who heaps up gains tew gloat over, iz like a hog in a pen, fatted for a show.

I hav finally cum tew the konklushun, if a man kant be born but once, he had better issue proposals tew hav it dun somewhare in Nu England.

It is only a step from cunning tew dishonesty, but it iz a step that a man iz liable at enny time to take.

I don't kno az i want to bet enny money, and give odds, on the man who iz alwus anxious tew pra out loud every chance he can git.

When a man duz a good turn just for the phun ov the thing, he haz got a grate deal more virtew in him than he iz aware ov.

Suckcess is quite often like falling oph from a log, a man kant alwus tell how he kum to did it.

The man whom yu kant git to write poetry, or tell the truth, until yu git him haff drunk ain't worth the investment—No, sir.

Munny makes munny. We all ov us take our korn to the ritch miller tew hav it ground.

Silence iz alwus safe.

Thare iz, now and then, a man who knows that he iz a phool; sutch a man iz a hard man tew cheat.

The more humble a man iz before God, the more he will be exalted,—the more humble he iz before men, the more he will git rode ruff shod.

If yu are going to giv a man enny thing, giv it to him cheerfully, and quick, don't make him git doun on hiz kneeze in front ov you, and listen to the 10 command-ments, and then yu giv him 5 cents.

MISCELLANEOUS.

A CASE OF MISTAKEN IDENTITY.

PATRICK MOLONEY (Irish !) made a deposit, and the teller handed him the signature book for his name. He wrote in it, and passed it back to the teller, who looked at the signature and read "Dennis O'Neal." "Why !" said the teller, "I thought your name was Patrick Moloney." "And sure it is that same," said Pat. "Then why did you write Dennis O'Neal?" said the teller. "And did I?" said Pat; "thin, bedad, I was writing the name of another man I was thinking about, jist." (This actually occurred.)

A CHINAMAN'S COLLATERAL.

This unique advertisement from a "Frisco" paper shows one beautiful side of the Chinese question.

"Wang Geu owes Dr. Yee Cheugh Five Hundred and Fifty Dollars. He cannot pay it. So, according to the Chinese law, he left his woman, Sing Gim, in Dr. Yee Cheugh's possession as collateral, until the money shall be paid. All right. By and by, all same yesterday, Sing Gim stole Three Hundred and Seventy Dollars from Dr. Yee Cheugh, and ran away. Now then all

[245]

Chinamen take notice that if you keep Sing Gim you must pay me Nine Hundred and Twenty Dollars, all same Wang Geu. 	Dr. Yee Cheugh."

It is to be hoped Dr. Y. C. recovered his money or his " stock."

HOW TO RESTORE CONFIDENCE.

National Bank, No. 2268, at Winona, Minn., sends us this good one :

During the panic of '73 one of the banks in this city, though perfectly solvent, had more calls from those holding certificates than was desirable, though every one was paid promptly. One day a man called with one of $300, and the person at the counter went to the safe, and took out a large package of bills, on the top of which were three *one thousand dollar notes.* He took the package to the counter and in sight of the person who held the $300 certificate, turned up one of the thousand dollar notes, then the next one, and said, "This is not the package I wanted," and put it aside. The next day the customer told all his neighbors there was no danger of *that bank,* as he saw a package six inches deep, *all thousand dollar bills.* It took, and was well circulated, which doubtless kept many small depositors satisfied.

THE RISE IN GOLD.

During the late war, when gold reached 240 per cent., a deaf and dumb man stepped into a broker's office in N. J., and inquired, by aid of slate and pencil, what they would pay for gold, and received the laconic reply, "240." He considered—went out—returned—considered, and finally determined to sell. He produced a small package from his pocket, and removing wrapper after wrapper, brought forth one gold dollar piece. He was handed two dollars and forty cents. With a puzzled look he asked, "What's that?" The reply was "Two dollars and forty cents—240 for gold." Beginning to comprehend that the broker really intended to offer the amount as the value of his gold, he became indignant, and sharply asked "What do you mean?" The broker answered, "Why, 240 per cent. for gold is two dollars and forty cents." He said, almost fiercely, "I want two hundred and forty dollars!" and went out, resenting a supposed attempt to swindle him. His hoarded gold went with him. He had watched the reports of the rise of gold, and failing to take in the idea of *per cent.*, his dollar had grown, in his eyes, to fifty dollars—a hundred —two hundred—and at two hundred and forty dollars, the excitement of inflation had culminated in fear to hold longer, and a determination to realize.

How many wiser men have as sadly failed to "realize" since the *fall* of gold!

———◆———

A GRANGER'S IDEA.

A cashier in Iowa reports the following as a specimen of the average "granger" in his county:

Old Edwin T. has an unlimited confidence in the integrity of bank officers. He bought, last year, a cottage organ, for which his note was duly given for $175, with interest at 10 per cent., payable six months after date, to which was attached a property statement, "worth in real estate $15,000, and personal $5,000." The note being received by this bank for collection, Edwin was notified, and in a short time he presents and delivers himself thus :

" Mr. R., I am unable to pay that note. You know the times are hard, hogs are bringing little or nothing, and I find it out of the question to pay it now ; but I want to make a proposition to you, or to the owner of the note : I have a friend who will let me have the money if they will *throw off the interest.* Now, Mr. R., I will pay you *one dollar* if you will write to them, relating all the facts, and advising them to accept my offer !"

The munificent proposition was respectfully declined.

Cashier *Speer* of Americus, Ga., incloses two incidents (true ones), and says the story as told by the simple old farmer was much more full of pathos and poetry, glowing thoughts, and burning words, than his reproduction of the same on paper, but " What is writ is writ, I would it were *more worthy*."

A HUMBLE INCIDENT.

How many romances in real life remain unwritten ? How many sweet idyls remain unsung ? How many

sons of toil have lived out their allotted days full of
bright hopes and grand aspirations, and "after life's
fitful fever they sleep well"? teaching us that we should
not despise "the short and simple annals of the poor."
There lived a few years ago, and may live there still, not
remote from Americus, Ga., an honest, hard-working
man, who had a little farm, a wife, and three "olive
plants" to cheer him onward in his daily toil, and after
the "former and latter rains," kind heaven "blessed him
in his basket and in his store." His cotton loaded on
his wagon for the morrow's departure, he and his wife
sat up late into the overnight, discussing and planning
what they should do after paying their debts, and as his
mother-in-law (the much persecuted relation) had
promised them a visit shortly, he must buy some new
but inexpensive furniture to adorn their humble home,
and as Christmas was near at hand, must not forget
"Santa Claus" in providing toys for the little ones. So
early morning found him far on his way to market, the
cotton sold, the check presented at bank and paid, but
unwittingly he leaves on the counter a fifty and a twenty
dollar bill, which the banker did not observe at the
time, and the man being a stranger to him, he could
only wait his return. He paid his debts and then discovered his loss. One of his friends suggested to him
to go back to the bank, that he might have left the
money there; he said no, he saw the money counted, it
was all right, so he "homeward wended his weary way,"
hope and joy gone, and sadness instead filled his heart.
His debts were paid, but nothing left to make bright and

11*

cheerful his home—his wife met him at the gate in full expectation of the treat in store for the little ones. What was her dismay? What could they do more than "hang their harps upon the willows" and "sit down by the ruins at Babylon and weep"?

It was some weeks before he returned to town and found that his money was safe. It was then he told the banker this story.

SHIFTING THE RESPONSIBILITY.

This episode in a banker's experience antedates the "late unpleasantness between the States"—in the good old days of free banking—State issues *ad infinitum*, the same transpiring on the day that the daily papers had made this announcement, "It is reported that the Bank of Columbus has suspended." Customer, in drawling tones, "Mr. S., I want you to take eight hundred dollars that I owe Mr. H., and give me your receipt for it." To expedite business, I wrote and handed him receipt for same. After deliberately reading it, folds it and puts it deep down in his capacious pocket; then slowly pulls out his wallet and hands over the money, in which there is a fifty dollar bill on the Bank of Columbus. His attention being called to the fact, he replies, in slow, measured words, "It is with you—you are responsible."

This is a list of what different people have asked us for when they wanted DEPOSIT TICKETS.

Depositing checks.	New blanks.
Depositing blanks.	Heads.
Lodgment blanks.	Backs.
Deposit stumps.	Pads.
Deposit slips.	Notices.
Deposit sheets.	Bills.
Deposit papers.	Tablets.
Deposit forms.	Statements.
Deposit stubs.	Evidences.
Deposit cards.	Dockets.
Deposit vouchers.	Documents.
Deposit heads.	Requisitions.
Record slips.	Scrip.
Entry checks.	Certificates.
Paying-in checks.	Minutes.
Paper lists.	Entries.
Check heads.	Slabs.
Credit tickets.	Blocks.
Listing sheets.	Tabs.
Blank forms.	Tags.
Slip books.	Notes.

AN ANECDOTE FROM MONTREAL.

Sandy B——, a Scotchman, who boasts of his wealth, was asked to join a club in this city. "Eh! mon, I canna afford it." "But, Mr. B——, you're as rich as

Crœsus." "Wall, I dunno who Crœsus is, but I'll plant dollar for dollar wuth um."

———◆———

I suppose you have heard of the man who went into a London bank, and pitching a plate upon a pile of sovereigns which were being weighed, answered the clerk's astonished look by saying, "a pound of butter, and be quick about it." The plate was carefully handed back, with the intimation that he was in the wrong shop; the man went off grumbling, and, when he got into a quiet corner was caught by a detective coolly picking off some five or six sovereigns which he had secured by carefully waxing the bottom of his plate before going for his butter.

———◆———

SUIT AGAINST THE QUEEN.

A queer case springs from the failure of the City of Glasgow Bank. A lady died recently having no heirs and leaving no will, and her property went to the Crown. Among her possessions was some of the stock, and as each shareholder is individually liable for the debts it is proposed to hold the Queen responsible! One bank which had taken four shares from a customer in its debt has been called upon to put its whole capital, £130,000, at the order of the directors who are winding up the Glasgow concern. At the last service which Mr. Lewis Pelly, one of the imprisoned directors, attended, the hymn was, "The hour of my departure's come," and it was sung to the ominous tune of "Duke Street."

SOLOMON'S ADVICE.

Just after the strike, when Solomon closed the discussion by telling the sluggard to go to the ant, the sluggard replied with a knowing wink, that he had a much softer thing than that. "As how?" inquired the proverbial monarch. "I will start a savings bank," replied the man of inertia. The monarch nodded slowly, twice or thrice, and went away to get shaved. The next time he met the sluggard that deliberate individual was riding in a gold-mounted carriage, with coachman and footman in livery, and in reply to the monarch's nod, he just pulled up to say that he was going over to Europe for a little while till the flurry blew over. And Solomon went back into his sanctum and wrote : "Better is an handful with quietness than a bank book as big as a Bible with travail and vexation of spirit."

THE BANK OF ENGLAND.

Mrs. Jane G. Swisshelm describes a visit to the Bank of England, and compares its dingy, almost shabby, appearance with the palatial banking houses erected in this country. She continues : "So long as the American people trust their money to folks because they have magnificent banking houses, or other places of business, splendid residences, retinues of servants, high-stepping horses, glittering coaches, flashing diamonds, gauzy laces, rustling silks, shimmering satins, and sweeping velvets, so long do they prove that they belong to that class of animated nature which was made to be eaten, and have no right to complain when the eaters eat them."

NOTHING BUT A BANKER.

Said a pompous man of money to Professor Agassiz : "I once took some interest in natural science ; but I became a banker, and I am what I am !"

" Ah !" replied Agassiz, " my father procured for me a place in a bank ; but I begged for one more year of study, then for a second, then for a third. That fixed my fate, sir. If it had not been for that little firmness of mine, I should now have been nothing but a banker."

THE VALUE OF COURTESY.

Stout, of the Shoe and Leather Bank, New York, is celebrated for his financial success, and for his inexhaustble good nature. He is never so busy but he has a kind word for the humblest. When they are rushing things in the bank, Mr. Stout always finds time to say, " Take a seat ; I'll be at leisure in a moment." A man came into the bank the other day and opened an account.

" I came here," he said, " not simply because I knew my money would be safe with you, but because you are always civil. I have been a depositor in ——— Bank for many years. I went in to-day to see the cashier. I knew him when he had no society to boast of, and hardly enough money to pay for a dinner in a cheap restaurant. I laid my hat on the desk, which I suppose I had no business to do. He waved his hand with an imperious air, and said, ' Take this hat off.'

"I removed my hat, when he said, 'Now I will hear what you have to say.'

"' I have nothing to say to you,' I replied.

"I went to the book-keeper, ordered my account to be made up, took the bank's check for $42,000, and this I wish to deposit."

The president and cashier represent two styles of business common in New York. Sauciness does not bear a high commercial value among the financial men of the city.

----◆----

A HEATHEN BANKER.

Muria Kimata, of Tokio, formed a company to lend money to the poor at low interest. It proved a failure, for though there were enough poor people anxious to borrow, few of them would repay their loans. Muria Kimata, therefore, had to abandon his project, having lost heavily himself, and involved many of his friends with him. A large fortune, however, still remained to him. On the anniversary of his father's death, he called the stockholders together, and out of his private means paid to each the amount of his loss ; then, placing their receipts, with all the obligations and securities given to the company by the poor borrowers, in a brazier, with incense, he burned them before the shrine of Hotoke Sama. Muria Kimata is a heathen idolater.

A CRAZY MAN'S DESPERATE LEAP.

[FROM THE TROY TIMES.]

A gentleman who had been cashier of a bank in a western city, by excessive labor and great domestic affliction became insane, and last Fall was sent to the water cure at Clifton Springs, with a constant attendant, for aid. For several weeks he occupied a room in the fourth story. One afternoon, as his attendant was in a doze in his chair, with the front window down at the top, he seized a pillow from the bed and threw it out of the window and immediately sprang after it, to the utter consternation of the attendant, who opened his eyes to see the glimpse of his patient passing out almost like a shot. Running down stairs as fast as his speed could make, to gather up the supposed mangled remains, he found the patient had "lit," so to speak, on the pillow on the piazza roof, some 30 feet below, and was not fatally injured, and still more remarkable was the fact that the shock brought him to his senses, and he has continued rational ever since.

AN INCIDENT OF RESUMPTION.

A well-preserved old gentleman entered the Sub-Treasury building on Wednesday, and presented 35 $1,000 called bonds for redemption. After the usual formalities had been gone through with and the necessary papers signed, the clerk placed upon the counter seven bags containing $5,000 each in gold coin. The old gentleman gasped out :

" Wha—wha—what's this ?"

"Your $35,000, sir," was the reply.

"But I don't want gold. Give me legal tenders. I am 74 years of age, and I can't carry those about with me," said the old gentleman, struggling to lift one bag.

"We have no authority to pay legal tenders, Sir. We are redeeming called bonds in gold."

The old gentleman expostulated, but in vain. He hurried to the Gallatin National Bank and begged President Tappen to get him out of his scrape. Mr. Tappen explained that all he could do would be to receive the gold on deposit and allow him to draw a check against it. The old gentleman was delighted. He said he did not care what the arrangement was so that he could obtain greenbacks instead of the gold. The bank's porter was sent after the bags, the deposit was made, the check drawn, and the old gentleman went on his way rejoicing.

SOME BONDS FIND THEIR OWNER AT LAST.

A singular incident in banking experience has happened in the course of the business transactions of Messrs. H. H. Hughes & Co., bankers in Cincinnati. Nine and a half years ago one Hugh Williams left 7-30 United States bonds to the amount of $1,200 to be exchanged for 5-20s. The bankers effected the exchange, but found that Mr. Williams had neglected to leave his address, and his name could not be found in the directories.   Time ran on and this special deposit was carried forward from year to year by the bankers for nine and a half years, and till quite recently.   Mr. Williams had completely disappeared.   Lately, on examining the record of special deposits a clerk remarked : " Where can Mr. Williams be ?"   Mr. Harry Hughes, overhearing the remark, said he had a classmate named Williams, who came from Paddy's Run, Butler County.   A friend (Rev. Mr. Chidlaw) who lived at Paddy's. Run, was written to, and he was asked if he happened to know one Hugh Williams.   He replied that Williams was his brother-in-law ; that he had been dead eight years ; that his estate had been settled up, and that there was no memorandum found among his papers showing the ownership of the bonds in question.   The executor of Hugh Williams came to the city recently, identified himself to Messrs. Hughes & Co., and received the bonds, to which were attached the coupons due since 1868.

THE PUZZLED DUTCHMAN.

Warp Borgman was as honest a young Dutchman as ever lived.   He had only worked with us a short time, say three months, and had not asked for any pay.   As he never used tobacco or went out with the boys I was not surprised.   However, the time came at last.   He wanted six dollars, and said :

" The year is about up when my interest is due on

the $100 I let Mr. Klinefetter have to keep for me, and I must pay him."

It took a great deal of time and patience to convince him that Klinefetter owed him $106—and no doubt he yet is in a mystery of fog, to know how a man can go to the expense of keeping up a safe, vault, building, clerks, book-keepers, &c., all for nothing, and then pay for a chance to take care of other people's money. Will some one write to him and explain ?

RUBBING OUT AN OLD SCORE.

About twenty-five years ago the undersigned, in partnership with an elderly gentleman by the name of Laning, began on a limited scale the mercantile business in the then village of Petersburg. Our store-room was a small concern about twenty by forty feet, and our daily sales did not exceed twenty-five dollars, the greater portion being on a credit of twelve months. My partner, Jacob Laning (familiarly known as " Uncle Jake ") was from New Jersey, a man small in stature but possessed of a clear business mind.

Among our country customers was one whom we will call " Bill Thomas," who was a continual source of annoyance. His trade in the course of a year did not amount to much, and yet he invariably beat us in every bargain, and what goods he did buy, he managed to get at less than first cost. Thomas was a close, slippery customer, full of blarney and flattery, and whose moral integrity was not above question.

After this state of things had existed for some years, we held a council of war one day and it was unanimously decided that Thomas was to suffer for some of his many misdeeds in our next transaction with him. We had not long to wait; standing in the front of our store one day we espied him coming into town. After some disputing as to which of us should tackle him, each claiming to have been the worst skinned by him, my partner being the elder, I succumbed, and took my position near the stove in company with Mr. Laning's eldest son, Ed., who came into the store just at this time. I told him that his father was going to "go for" Bill Thomas, who would be in the store in a few minutes. Enter Thomas. "How do you do, Uncle Jake: you don't seem to get any older. I believe you are better and younger looking every time I see you. Do you buy furs here, Uncle Jake?" Here was a stunner. We never had dealt any in furs, and Uncle Jake was as ignorant of their value as a hog is of logarithms, but fearing he might lose this opportunity to shave Thomas, he said:

"Well, I don't know, Bill, what have you?"

"Two fine possum skins," said he, producing the pelts of two of the smallest specimens of the opossum family. "They offered me twenty-five cents a piece for these over yonder, but as I like you, and do all my trading with you, I will let you have them at twenty cents each." The trade was soon consummated, and now for the bargain in which Uncle Jake was to clear "old scores." After striving in vain to sell him a bill, he was beginning to despair, when Thomas spied the tobacco box.

"How do you sell these plugs, Uncle Jake?" This tobacco was as staple at 25 cents per plug as calico or domestic was at the same price in those days.

"This tobacco is worth 25 cents a plug, Bill, and can't be bought for any less in town."

"Oh, Uncle Jake, now you can let me have them for 20 cents apiece."

"No, I can't, Bill, they cost that."

"See here now, Uncle Jake. I sold you my furs under price, and you must let me have these two plugs for my furs." After haggling for some time, Thomas won the day, Uncle Jake thinking to get him started once, and go for him on something he was not posted in. But Bill was too smart for him, and would not bite for another cent's worth, and went on his way rejoicing.

We could hold in no longer, but burst into shouts of laughter at the way in which the old man had been sold. We joked him a great deal, and told all the jokers in town of it, and it was a long time till he heard the last of it.

That night his son Ed. (who, by the way, was one of the worst boys in town) and I cut the legs off of one side of both skins and rubbed a little dirt over them, and the next morning showed them to him and said :

"See here, Thomas cut one skin in two, and sold it to you for two skins," placing them side by side, making them look like one.

"That's so ; by George, I never saw such a rascal in all my life. The skins were not worth five cents apiece."

After the lapse of seventeen years, I went into the banking business here, in partnership with the Hon. Wm. G. Greene, one of the wealthiest old farmers in the county ; the style of the firm was Brahm and Greene. I had always told Mr. Laning I intended some day to make Bill Thomas pay him the forty cents he swindled him out of in the " opossum skin trade."

Not long since, Thomas came into the bank to borrow forty dollars on 60 days' time. I told him times were hard, money scarce, and upon the whole I could not let him have it. He insisted very strongly, and offered good security. Said I, " Bill, you are getting along in years now, and you ought to fix that matter up with Uncle Jake ; you ought not to die with that item charged up against you."

" Now, Brahm, you must ' take a rest ' on that old joke ; you have told it to every man in the county."

He kept insisting on my letting him have the money, and I finally said : "If you will pay Uncle Jake that 40 cents and interest at 10 per cent., Bill, I will let you have the money." After demurring a while, he finally agreed, and I made him the loan, and kept out $2.03, the amount due Uncle Jake on the "opossum skin trade." After he left the bank, I went in search of Mr. Laning, and told him I had collected the 40 cents off of Bill, with the interest. He at first refused to receive the money, but I insisted that he should take it, as Thomas justly owed it, and it would spoil a good story, if he didn't keep it, to which he at last agreed.

JOHN A. BRAHM,
of the firm of
Brahm & Greene,
Petersburg,
Illinois.

DEATH IN LIFE.

The other day I heard a cabinet minister talking to a young chap who wanted a place.

"My young friend," said he, "don't apply. Saw wood, drive cows, anything honorable, but preserve your independence. I have a man in my department who has been in forty years."

" Forty years ?"

" Yes, every day of it. He came in in 1836. Well, he gets about the same salary he had to commence with. The other day he came to me, saying : 'I ought to have died forty years ago.' 'You don't mean that,' I said. 'Yes,' said he, 'I mean that I have been buried in this building forty years, and I had just as well been buried in the grave. What's the difference between tombs? Of what advantage have I been to myself in here? I had nothing when I came in, and have got nothing now. I am disqualified for anything. If I were turned out to-day, I would starve to-morrow.' So much for a government position, or a banker's clerkship, that young men are so anxious to obtain. They had better let it alone."

"THAT'S MY NAME."

A man forty years old, and as long as a rail, went into one of the banks of Detroit to get the cash on a thirteen dollar check, drawn by a party living in Nankin township.

"You will have to be identified," said the cashier, as he looked at the check.

"I'm the man," was the reply.

"But I don't know who you are."

"But I do."

"You must bring some one here who knows you."

"Don't I know myself?" exclaimed the check tenderer.

"But I must know you. You may be Tom Jones for all that I know."

"You must be a consarned fool to think I'm some one else," growled the man in response.

"You must be identified," observed the cashier.

"That's my name, I tell ye, and this is me, and if this bank gets me riled, I'll lick the whole crowd of you over behind the railing!"

The cashier wouldn't pay, and the man couldn't find any one who knew him, and at noon he was waiting "for the feller who sassed him to come out."

A SMART CLERK.

Adolph Z. is young, not unprepossessing, and a clerk in a wealthy banker's office in Paris, on a salary of $600 a year. The banker has a pretty daughter of eighteen. Adolph has not a cent, but that does not deter him from waiting upon his employer one morning, and saying : "Sir, I have the honor of asking your daughter's hand in marriage." The banker, astonished, rang the bell, and told the waiter to throw Adolph out of the window. "As you please," calmly said the young clerk, "but before that is done learn that I am about to become a partner in the London house of Bathurst & Co." At this the banker softens. "The proof, sir, the proof of what you say." "Give me forty-eight hours in which to go to England, and I will bring you the proof." Adolph hurries to London, presents himself at the office of Bathurst & Co., and says : "I have come to propose that you take me as a partner," and, as Mr. Bathurst looks as though he thought Adolph demented, he adds : "I am about to marry the daughter of M. P., of Paris." Adolph is thereupon asked to be seated, they converse, and come to terms. The bright young man returns to Paris, carrying to his future father-in-law the proof of his statement, and the young people are wedded.

VANDERBILT'S RULE FOR GETTING RICH.

The New York *Tribune* has the following : Commodore Vanderbilt seemed to be in an unusually communicative mood, for he made the following suggestions to the reporter : "When you have lived, sir, to carry as many gray hairs as I do, you will have learned that there is little sympathy with, or appreciation of your efforts, it matters little what may be the circumstances. If you are successful in accumulating a fortune, you will be called a speculator and a monopolist, while, if you should fail to amass riches, it will all be about the same, as you will be talked of, in that case, as one who does not amount to much anyhow. I have never speculated on the market, and regard it as nothing less than a gambling operation. When I was thirty years old, I had been working, for several years, for my employer, at $1,000 a year, and when I left him I had not more than $2,000, all told."

"After a long and very successful life, Commodore, what, in your opinion, is the true secret of success in making money?"

"Save what you have and live within your income. Avoid all speculation. No matter what I was making, I always made it a rule to save something, and this course, if persisted in, is sure to succeed. The money will pile up in time."

CONVICT SPECULATORS.

HOW CALIFORNIA CONVICTS TURN HONEST PENNIES.

A correspondent of the San Francisco *Chronicle*, writing from San Quentin, where the California State Prison is situated, says :

"Many prisoners have accumulated considerable sums of money by their overwork and the sale of fancy articles manufactured during their leisure. Others are possessed of means, and carry on a general banking business in the prison, loaning to their fellow-convicts at San Quentin, at rates of interest which vary through a wide range. Recently one of the officers was called to

POPULAR PICTURES.

THE BANK CLERK OFF DUTY.—*Page* 267.

arbitrate concerning a demand for $17 made by one
prisoner upon another. The debtor denied a greater
liability than $5, whereupon the exacting creditor ex-
plained the discrepancy by stating that his rate of interest was ten per centum a day, and the debt had been
running some weeks. The officer pronounced the demand disgraceful to the San Quentin bourse, and
declined to urge its acknowledgment."

POPULAR PICTURES—THE BANK CLERK.

As you enter the bank he is standing in a statuesque
position against the walnut counter, gazing dreamily
through the thick plate glass into the street. You have
come to make a deposit, and you want to do it in a
hurry, as you live out of town, and there isn't more than
enough time to catch the boat. So when you see that
he is still busily watching a young lady who is getting
out of a stage, you cough, and tap on the window.
Presently he becomes vaguely aware that some one
needs his attention. The smile that has been playing
about his natty mustache goes off to play somewhere
else, and the frown of business takes its place. "Come,
now, hurry up," he says, "can't wait for you all day,"
and he says it so honestly that you are forced into beg-
ging his pardon, and have that depreciating opinion of
yourself which almost prompts you to tender him a
cigar. He takes your book, flips it upside down on the
counter, seizes the ticket with the second motion of the

arm, and is about to impale it on his file when he notices
that you haven't written the date in. He hands it back,
and waves you to a dark desk in the corner of the room,
which is designed for the use of the public. Such being
the case, it is quite natural that there should be no pens
there. When at last you borrow a pen from the note-clerk,
whom you know slightly, you find that there is no ink
in the stand. All this time they are ringing the first bell
of the boat, and you are rendered desperate by a knowledge of the fact. Finally the date is written, you rush
back, and have to take your place at the tail end of a line
which has formed during your absence. In such cases
there is always some man before you who wants interest
calculated, or who wishes to know the collection charge
on Oshkosh, having in his deposit a greasy draft for $11
on that far-away spot. Just as your time comes, and you
get your hand through the window, the clerk recollects
that he wants a drink of water. So he goes over to the
cooler, drinks calmly and deliberately, and stops on his
way back to ask Jenkins, one of the bookkeepers, who it
is that is going to play "short stop" on the occasion of
the coming match with the Accident Insurance Club.
The result is evident. You miss your boat, have to stay
in town all night, to find, the next day, that your wife is
in tears and her bonnet, determined to go home to her
mother ; or you rush madly out of the bank, get stopped
at the corner by a policemen, who is sure that you have
a package of stolen bonds under your coat ; explain ex-
citedly, to the amusement of the crowd ; rush on down
to the wharf, and get hauled on board by two of the

deck hands, just as the boat is moving into the stream, only to remember, when you are a hundred feet from shore, that you forgot to have a note extended, and that it will be sent to protest in the morning.

This kind of clerk is quite an elegant individual. He dresses nicely, wears rings, and parts his hair in the middle. He always rides up and down town in a stage, consults the Stock Exchange tape when he goes to lunch, and firmly believes that he will yet make a colossal fortune on the street. Sometimes he tries to declare a larger dividend than the bank, and, in such cases, it is not unlikely that he buys a ticket for out West, and takes to driving mules on the plains. Or he may run over to Europe for his health. If he happens to be a paying teller, he is still more dignified than the gentleman who receives your money. You present a check to him. He takes it, turns it over, looks at the indorsement, compares the signature with the one in the depositors' register, looks at you, then glances over in the corner to see that the bank detective is at his post, and finally asks you how you will have it. "In fives and twenties, if you please," you say. So he gives you tens and fifties. You take the money without a word, and are conscious that you are leaving the bank with a guilty air, and that the teller's eye is on you.

There never was yet a bank without its patriarchal clerk. He is always small, always bent at the shoulders, always wears glasses, always sits on a preposterously high stool, is gray headed, speaks in a squeaky voice, and invariably has a cold, and a gigantic red handkerchief for its accommodation. The junior clerks have a legend among them that he was left as a foundling on the bank steps eighty years ago, and has been with the institution ever since. He is first at the bank in the morning, sitting on his stool, and the last at night, still sitting on his stool. He never goes out to lunch, but nibbles at a bit of cheese which he keeps in a dark drawer. It is sometimes believed that he never leaves the house, but sleeps at night in the iron safe, curled up on one of the gigantic ledgers. But this is a mere rumor.

With all his peculiarities, the bank clerk is not a bad fellow. He recognizes, of course, that fate has arrayed him against society, and it is only necessary to remember this fact in order to excuse his *brusquerie*. His life is a monotonous one. At ten o'clock his window opens with a click ; at three o'clock it closes with a bang ; and between those hours he is busy counting dirty bank notes, answering idiotic questions, adding up gigantic columns of figures, watching the young ladies in the street, and consulting the ledgers. Outside the window are the lines of depositors, check drawers, and other varieties of bank customers. He has to keep a keen watch for counterfeit money and forged signatures, and—for the young ladies. When we reflect, then, how difficult it is for a young man to count a package of notes half of which are upside down, or examine a signature written by a depositor the morning after a wine supper, and at the same time miss no dainty promenader on Broadway, if such be the street, we can appreciate the laboriousness of the situation, and agree with him that he is an ill-used and much underpaid individual.

—*New York Evening Post.*

———◆———

Brother Coffin, Cashier Richmond National Bank, Indiana, contributes the following good ones for our million readers :

A WRONG COUNT.

DIALOGUE.

Farmer (who has been paid parcel of $500, duly banded and proved). See here! this yere parcel ain't right.

Teller. Oh, I guess it is—have you counted it?

Farmer. Well, I reckon I have. I counted it four times.

Teller. What did you make it?

Farmer. Why, I made it $490, $485, $495, and $505, and I *know* it ain't right.

LIGHT. WEIGHT.

A rare old examiner was Judge Samuel Perkins, first president of the State Bank of Indiana. On his first visit of inspection to the Richmond Branch, he found its reserve fund (silver coin was the sole reserve of those days) all put up in kegs. Slowly and painfully he counted the contents of one keg. Night was approaching. "Well," says he, "I'll 'heft' the balance;" so he proceeded to "heft" them, and announced that one keg was evidently short weight. It was duly opened and counted, and found to be *short twenty-five cents.*

THE BANK THAT LASTED A DAY.

A few years ago, an old German living at Hamilton, Ohio, who had accumulated wealth by hard labor, thought he would enjoy the *ease* of the banking business, with its well-known freedom from care, and rapid accumulation of wealth, so he opened out an office in due form. The first customer applied for a loan of $500. After a prodigious amount of investigation, and on receipt of undoubted security, the loan was duly made. The second customer appeared with a like request. This excited our worthy friend to a high degree, and he answers hotly that he has already made one loan, and "by Gosh!" he wants to see if that is paid before he loans any more. The next customer wanted "change for a ten," and was duly accommodated in haste; what was the chagrin of our worthy friend, to discover a few minutes later that it was a base counterfeit; saddened and disgusted with his experience, he closed his doors at night and abandoned the business forever.

THIS is a fine passage of Paulding's :

"Nothing is more easy than to grow rich. It is only to trust nobody, befriend no one; to heap interest upon interest, cent upon cent; to destroy all the finer feelings of nature, and be rendered mean, miserable, and despised for some twenty or thirty years, and riches will come as sure as disease, disappointment, and a miserable death."

THE ALMIGHTY DOLLAR.

Harper's Drawer puts upon record, for the information of its hundreds of thousands of readers, the name of the author of that humorous phrase that now passes current in the wit of both hemispheres, " *The Almighty Dollar.*" The expression originated with Washington Irving, in " The Creole Village."

" *The Almighty Dollar*, that great object of universal devotion throughout our land, seems to have no devotees in these peculiar villages."

In the last edition of Mr. Irving's works, in a footnote, he says : " This phrase, used for the first time in this sketch, has since passed into current circulation, and by some has been questioned as savoring of irreverence. The author, therefore, owes it to his orthodoxy to declare that no irreverence was intended, *even to the dollar itself,* which he is aware is daily becoming more and more an object of worship."

SOMETIMES EASILY MISTAKEN.

A well-to-do farmer having purchased a draft at his banker's, and days and weeks having elapsed without
12*

having received any acknowledgment of same, he writes to his friends for an explanation. In due time, he is informed that the draft had never been received, and advised to go to the bank immediately and obtain a duplicate. He goes to the bank and makes known his business. After the cashier had asked the usual questions as to the possibility of his letter having been misdirected, unstamped, &c., &c., the farmer very promptly replied that his mind was clear as to the correctness of *his* part of the business, and that he *remembered very distinctly* of having purchased the draft, and writing his letter then and there, inclosing it with draft in a stamped envelope, addressing it properly, and *depositing it in the Post Office himself*.

"Now," says he, "the money has never reached its destination, and I will show you a letter from the parties to whom the draft was sent;" and, in reaching into his pocket for the letter, he accidentally pulls out the one containing the draft, which he was so *positive* of having mailed. Farmer wilts.

"REVOLUTION TAX."

During the late war, when the government was taxing its citizens on their annual incomes, a gentleman who was not an extensive reader of political economy, and whose income for the past year had come within the limits of the law, went to his county town for the purpose of paying his tax. After looking around for the proper officer to receive his money, he came across a National Bank, which he thought might be the proper place to receive revenue taxes, so he entered the bank, and walking up to the teller's window, in a very patriotic manner inquired if that was the place to pay the "*Revolution Tax.*" Another inquiring genius called on us the other day for a marriage license.

------◆------

WANT OF "EDDICATION."

An honest farmer called at a bank and paid a collection note of $32. Soon he called again, and said he had lost a $10 bill. Teller had found no error, nor any stray $10. Farmer then said he must have dropped it at the warehouse, half a mile away. Thither he trudged, through a cold December rain, and mud ankle-deep. Returned in an hour or two, wet and chilled. No success. Teller finally concluded to question him. How much money had you when you came to town? Ans. $17. How much was paid to you at the warehouse? Ans. $25. How much have you now in your pocket? Ans. (mournfully) *Only* $7. I must have dropped a $10 bill somewhere, he repeated. Well, says the teller,

You had in the morning	$17
You received at the warehouse	25
Making	$42
You paid me . . $32	
You have on hand . 7 Making	39
Leaving you short only . . .	$3

The farmer felt better, and concluded he would not tramp around any more in the rain and mud looking for that, which, after all, might be in his pocket. So much for the want of a little idea of figuring.

WATCH HOW YOUR CUSTOMERS SPIT.

A stranger enters an Ohio bank, and presents a check, which is cashed. He carefully counts over the money, and very adroitly manages to let a large bill fall upon the floor unseen to the teller.

The teller is informed that the money is short, and takes it back, and while he is testing the correctness of his former count, his customer has *occasion* to spit, and in doing so, the teller notices the eyes of the stranger somewhat riveted upon the floor.

Mr. Teller's suspicions being somewhat aroused, immediately leaves his window, and starts for the outside of the counter, and as he passes through the gate, Mr. Stranger is seen picking up the missing bill, who concludes the count was all right, after all. His excuse for spitting upon the floor for the purpose of seeing exactly where the bill was located, so that it could be transferred to his pocket, was detected just in time to save a "cash short $10" at night.

PLATE-GLASS SPITTOONS.

An agriculturalist, whose eyes had become somewhat dimmed by age, being in a bank one day, and while talking with the cashier, he had accumulated an extra amount of tobacco juice, and after his mouth was so full that he could talk no longer, he concluded to relieve his distress; so he walked up to a fine plate-glass window, and supposing there was no glass, he braced himself, and throwing forward his head, he gave one tremendous blast that completely covered the glass with the beautiful liquid, and the farmer with mortification.

----◆----

TRAPPING ROGUES WITH SUNSHINE.

The London *News* reports that the Bank of France has for some time past employed a photographic detective to examine suspicious documents, and more recently has placed an invisible studio in a gallery behind the cashiers. Hidden behind some heavy curtain, the camera stands ready for work, and at a signal from any of the cashiers, the photographer secures the likeness of any suspected customer. It is also reported, that in the principal banking establishment in Paris several frauds have lately been detected by the camera, which, under some circumstances, exercises a sharper vision than the human eye. Where an erasure has been made, for instance, the camera detects it at once, let the spot be ever so smoothly rubbed over, while a word or figure that to the eye has been perfectly scratched out, is clearly reproduced in a photograph of the document.

----◆----

WHAT IT WAS WORTH.

A Buffalo gentlemen who owns a $100 bond of the "City" of Neosho Falls, Ks., recently wrote to the local treasurer as to its value. He received the following reply : " Take the bond to a store and weigh it ; then find a market report containing the quotation of waste paper, and you will know the value of your bond."

SINGULAR BIBLE CLASS.

James McCormick, a millionaire bank president in Harrisburg, Pa., teaches a remarkable Bible class. There are 300 members, of whom he says : " There are men in this class who are by no means Christians ; men who are not even reformed. One of the worst gamblers in this city is a regular attendant. He is a bad man, and confesses it, but there's a spark of goodness in his heart, which, some day, may be fanned into a flame."

A BANKER'S LOVE OF BIRDS—GIRARD'S LITTLE SONGSTERS.

The smallest means of adding to his fortune were never neglected or overlooked by Girard. To him nothing was a trifle, if a penny could be made by it.

His breed of *canary birds* was among the most choice and extensive in the world, and he was careful to sell them at the highest price. The fondness of Girard for these little creatures was remarkable; he had his favorites among them, and doubtless enjoyed many a happy moment under the influence of the music of their songs— a sweet and singular solace from the distractions of trade, and which seemed to indicate, after all, a native trait of tenderness lurking at the bottom of his heart. True, he sold them, and they contributed to gratify his superlative passion in that way; but it would be ungenerous to suppose that he was not susceptible to feelings of delight from those winsome strains of melody which, at the same time, naturally commanded so high a price in the market.

A MILLIONAIRE ON GIVING AWAY MONEY : PETER C. BROOKS.

Peter C. Brooks, one of New England's most noted millionaires, made it a systematic practice to give away considerable sums of money, both for public and private purposes, though always in the same way that he did everything else, namely, without any parade. It appeared from his books that he annually expended in this way large amounts, but known at the time only to " Him who seeth in secret." He remarked to one of his sons, not long before his death, that " of all the ways of disposing of money, giving it away is the most satisfactory."

A WARNING.

The following was found written on the back of a bank note:

DRUNKARDS, TAKE HEED!

"When this note passes from me I am a ruined man. It is the last out of a fortune bequeathed to me, and the hard-won earnings of an indulgent parent—as quickly come, as quickly gone ; for after a few short years of inebriety and reckless folly, my dissipation has made me homeless, friendless and a beggar. Whoever may be the next owner of this note, I would recommend him to follow the advice of sad experience, and beware of intemperance."

————◆————

SHARING IN ROTHSCHILD'S FORTUNE.

During the stormy days of 1848, two stalwart mobocrats entered the bank of the late Baron Anselm Rothschild, at Frankfort. "You have millions on millions," said they to him, "and we have nothing, you must divide with us." "Very well, what do you suppose the firm of Rothschild is worth?" "About forty millions of florins." "Forty millions, you think, eh? Now then, there are forty millions of people in Germany ; that will be a florin apiece. Here's yours."

HIS ANNUAL.

Little English, the book-black, having observed the annual statement of the police, letter carriers, insurance companies, banks, and so on, decided that it would be in order to give the public some statistics regarding his own profession. He has therefore compiled the following :-

Paid up capital	34c.
Surplus	6c.
No. of "blacks" during 1878 . .	1,461
Cash lost on street	$1 20
No. of fights	28
No. of victories	27
Present liabilities	02c.
Dividends to stockholders . . .	000.

HOW TO BE FAMOUS.

Said an ambitious wife to her slow-going husband the other day : " Why can't you distinguish yourself in some way ? Better be a great defaulter than nothing !"

"OLD JONES," the great Manchester banker, had his bank adjoining his tea warehouse, and he used to spend his leisure in straightening bent tea-chest nails.

Bankers ! Have the courage to tell a man why you refuse to discount his paper.

HAND-WRITING.

A correspondent of the Charleston (S. C.) *News and Courier* proposes that every citizen who now has the right to vote shall be enrolled, but that hereafter nobody shall be put on the list unless he can write his own name in the register in a legible hand. Goodness gracious! What a sweeping disfranchisement of bank presidents, cashiers, legislators, preachers, lawyers, merchants, in fact, everybody but the nicest sort of clerkly people, this would be! How could such men as Horace Greeley, Rufus Choate, or our eminent friend, General Spinner, ever expect to vote under such a law?

THE SCHOOLMASTER ABROAD.

Our bank had occasion to have a book-case and a few shelves put up, and this is the bill rendered :

Norfolk, v. a.

Det to Daniel young
For one Cobbert and foure
shelvs and 1 Cloths hors
And lumber to make them
With six dollars, 25 cts. $6.25
pade
D. young.

ROTHSCHILD'S HAPPINESS.

"You must be a happy man, Mr. Rothschild," said a gentleman who was sharing the hospitality of his splendid home, as he glanced at the more than regal sumptuousness of the appointments of the mansion.

"Happy! me happy!" was the reply. "What! happy, when just as you are going to dine, you have a letter placed in your hand, saying, 'If you don't send me £500, I will blow your brains out?' Happy! me happy!"

And the fact that he frequently slept with loaded pistols at the side of his gilded bed, is comment enough upon the happiness of the richest man on the face of the globe.

THE TWO BILLS.

A FABLE FOR THE CHILDREN.

Two bills were waiting in the bank for their turn to go out into the world. One was a little bill, only one dollar; the other was a big bill, a thousand-dollar-bill.

While lying there side by side, they fell a-talking about their usefulness. The dollar-bill murmured out:

"Ah, if I were as big as you, what good I would do! I could move in such high places, and people would be so careful of me, wherever I should go! Everybody would admire me, and want to take me home with them;

but, small as I am, what good can I do ?   Nobody cares
much for me.   I am too little to be of any use."

"Ah, yes ! that is so," said the thousand-dollar-bill ;
and it haughtily gathered up its well-trimmed edge that
was lying next the little bill, in conscious superiority.
"That is so," it repeated. "If you were as great as I
am, a thousand times bigger than you' are, then you
might hope to do some good in the world."   And its
face smiled a·wrinkle of contempt for the little dollar-
bill.

Just then the cashier comes, takes the little murmur-
ing bill, and kindly gives it to a poor widow.

"God bless you !" she cries, as with a smiling face
she receives it.   "My dear, hungry children can now
have some bread."

A thrill of joy ran through the little bill as it was
folded up in the widow's hand ; and it whispered, "I
may do some good, if I am small."   And, when it saw
the bright faces of· her fatherless ·children, it was very
glad that it could do a little good.

Then the little dollar-bill began its journey of usefulness.   It went first to the baker's for bread, then to
the miller's, then to the farmer's, then to the laborer's,
then to the doctor's, then to the minister's ; and, wherever it went, it gave pleasure, adding something to their
comfort and joy.

At last, after a long, long pilgrimage of usefulness
among every sort of people, it came back to the bank
again, crumpled, defaced, ragged, softened, by its daily
use.   Seeing the thousand-dollar-bill lying there, with

scarcely a wrinkle or a finger-mark upon it, it exclaims :

"Pray, sir, and what has been your mission of usefulness ?"

The big bill sadly replies, " I have been from safe to safe among the rich, where few could see me, and they were afraid to let me go out far, lest I should be lost. Few indeed are they whom I have made happier by my mission."

Then the little dollar-bill said, " It is better to be small, and go among the multitudes doing good, than to be so great as to be imprisoned in the safes of the few." And it rested satisfied with its lot.

MORAL.—The doing well of little every-day duties makes one the most useful and happy.   A. H.

LOSS BY ATTRITION.

As gold coin ages in wear, by attrition it becomes lighter, until it loses a portion of its value. Of course there is a point at which every sovereign becomes thus of too light weight. Last year the Bank of England weighed 23,100,000 sovereigns, of which 840,000 were rejected as too light. When a coin has nearly reached the point to which reference is made, even the slight attrition of being carried in a box will finish the work. It has been found that in a box of 5,000 sovereigns, all of legal weight when packed, after having been jolted in sending a few hundreds of miles, an average of *eight* of the number will be found to have turned the point while on the journey.

* * *

THE COST OF REVERSING AN OLD PROVERB.

Several years ago, a safe in the office of Samuel B. Clexton, a wool dealer of Troy, N. Y., was blown open by burglars and $2,000 stolen. Mr. Clexton had the safe repaired, but has kept it unlocked ever since, saying that he did not want to be at the expense of repairing it a second time, should burglars choose to call on him. Last night several burglars availed themselves of Mr. Clexton's economical precautions, and emptied the safe again, taking stocks and notes of the value of $20,000. Of course they did not injure the safe. Mr. Clexton has taken the precaution to stop payment on the stolen securities.

* * *

A SAFE PLACE FOR SECURITIES.

Old John Walsh was a banker, and also a money-lender. He was accounted a greedy, close-fisted old chap, yet he possessed a sort of grim, rigid humor, which, in some cases, was really funny. One day a dashing, reckless young man of the period called upon him. "Mr. Walsh," said he, "I want to borrow five hundred." "For how long?" "Six months." "What security can you give me?" The young fellow drew himself proudly up. "My own personal security, sir," he replied, with a flourish. Old John turned and opened a stout iron chest by his side. "Get in here, sir," said he. The young blade looked first at the chest and then at Walsh. "What for?" asked he. "Because here is where I always keep all of my personal securities."

———————◆———————

ABOVE WORK.

It is a pleasant thing to be lazy. The delightful sensation of having nothing to do, or still better, of having something to do, but resolutely setting yourself not to do it. To sit still on the hotel balcony, with your feet braced against the railing, and listen to your neighbor, an honest, busy man, worth a thousand of you, say, "Well, I must get down to the office," and pity him.

Pity him, as he walks briskly away to earn more money in four hours than you could spend in a week.

I am here to pity just such men. I do feel sorry for them. I think that sympathetic tears gather in my eyes as I watch my new friend hurry off to the bank, and think he has to stay there six mortal hours, and protest notes and compute interest. and shake his head over dubious paper, and smile sadly when the names of feeble indorsers are tendered him, and look icily pitiless when somebody wants an extension, and look awfully blank when he just goes whistling out of the bank and gets the extension anyhow, on the American plan. Why, I do feel sorry for my friend, and I wring his hand when next I meet him, and wish he could change places with me for a little while, and have a good time.

True, his income is more in a day than mine in a week. It is also true that his income keeps booming all the time, while my salary gently. but firmly stops when I do, but then, bless you, I have the best time.

Because he cares about things and people, and I don't care a continental. After I once get the general hours for meals fixed in my mind, the hotel becomes a haven of rest, earth is a paradise, people are good-natured, kind, and confiding, and the trail of the serpent is only found in the menagerie. I think I shall join the communists ; they appear to have about the easiest, most satisfactory view of things. Having nothing of my own to divide, I want to divide with everybody else. Generous man ; send me the chromo.

By the way, did you ever notice how peculiarly bewildering to the untrained mind are mercantile forms? The other day, being in a communistic mood, I had occasion to "divide" with the office. I had a vague idea how the thing ought to be done, in a general way, so I went into a bank and asked for a sight draft. Should the obliging cashier fill it out for me? I thanked him haughtily, and filled it up myself. I had my misgivings, but I handed it over.

The obliging cashier smiled.

"Do you wish us to collect this ?" he asked.

I said "yes," in the tones which I imagined Mr. Vanderbilt employed on similar occasions, and to my unspeakable amazement the obliging cashier said :

" Very well, sir, just leave the money with us, and we will remit it to your house at once."

And then I saw that, somehow or other, I had made the thing out just that way, and had drawn upon myself in favor of the office for three weeks' salary, during which time the office had not heard from me.

: There's too much "bigod nonsense" about these banks, anyhow.   —*Burdette.*

UNIQUE BANKING.

A Dutchman read somewhere that money doubled itself, by compound interest, every fourteen years, if it was put carefully away, and left untouched. The guileless Hollander at once dug a hole in the cellar, and buried four hundred dollars, packed in a tea-kettle. This was fourteen years ago last Wednesday. On that day he rose at four o'clock in the morning, and dug up his cash, with the confident expectation that it had increased to eight hundred dollars. His disappointment was great, and when his friends talk to him about mathematics now, he expresses the opinion that "Dem arithmetics ish all a lie !"

FATE OF A COMPOUND NOTE.

A compound interest note for $210 was received at the Treasury, on Saturday, for redemption. It was torn into a thousand bits, and the explanation accompanying

13

it is rather odd. It belonged to a German named Schlalagel, who, a short time ago, was committed to the poorhouse in Burlington, Coffee county, Kansas, as a pauper. In a few days thereafter he was found to be insane, and recently drowned himself in a well. After his death this note was found in his room, torn into almost numberless fragments, not one of which was missing. He had been carrying the note on his person for years.

A PEANUT PEDDLER'S SAVINGS BANK.

A poorly-clad girl lately went into the First National Bank of Troy, N. Y., and deposited $400. The teller suspected her of stealing the money, and gave notice to the police. The girl was subsequently arrested. When she asked what was charged against her, she was told that a telegram had been received from New York, accusing a person of her description of stealing money. The girl immediately acknowledged herself guilty, and gave the details of the robbery. She gave her real name, and said her father was a pea-nut peddler in New York, and for several years had treated her with systematic brutality. One day, after he had given her a severe beating, she was engaged in cleaning the floor of his room, when she discovered under the bed an old pair of trousers, in one leg of which, sewed in between the lining and the cloth, she found the $400. She took it and fled to Troy. She was lodged in jail, and her father was informed of her arrest.

GRANDEST INSTANCE OF DEBT.

The grandest instance of growing debt upon record is that of the King of Leon, mentioned by Mariana. Ferdinand Gonzalves had sold this prince a falcon upon credit. The interest was high, and it compounded itself in the course of a few years into a sum so enormous that the king was forced to make over to Gonzalves his rights on the kingdom of Castile, to be quit of the liability.

JOHN SHERMAN'S PLAN OF LIFE.

In a letter from a gentleman in public life, who has known John Sherman from infancy, occurs the following passage: "John Sherman started in life as a long, gawky lad, quiet and determined in manner, economical, and not easily turned aside when he had made up his mind to anything. He has always been a shrewd financier and naturally a money-making man, never, he believes, making a mistake in his calculations about investments. He made it a rule that he must each year lay aside at least $500, and regulated his expenditures in conformity with that determination. He never failed to do it, and when he saw his $500 safely invested then he used more, if there was more, for pleasure, or was more liberal in expenses. About six years after he began practice he was able to start the sash and blind factory which he saw was needed, and that was worth to him about $5,000 a year for about six years. It paid him in all about $30,000.

Almost every dollar he has to-day was made when he was a private citizen, or as the result of investments made during that time. He has very little to show for his long years of public life or since he has been paid a salary." This is perhaps intended as an authoritative denial of the charge that Sherman became rich while in office and on a small salary.

———————————————————————————

TREATMENT OF INSOLVENTS BY THE BANK OF ENGLAND.

As soon as an English house has failed, the Bank of England picks out the bills accepted by that firm, and returning them to the house from whom it has *received* them, demands instanter the amount, less the discount for the time they have to run. As the law does not recognize this proceeding, nor furnish any means for compelling acquiescence in the demand, it is quite optional with the indorser to comply with it or not ; but if he does not comply, or makes even a momentary hesitation in handing bank-notes for the undue bills bearing his indorsement, his credit with the bank is ended, his discount account closed, and the best and easiest source of obtaining accommodation cut off. Under these circumstances, the unfortunate merchant will make strenuous exertions to uphold his standing in such an important quarter.

FRACTIONAL CURRENCY.

Men who are hard-up want to be let a-loan.

———

How to meet a man of doubtful credit.—Take no note of him.

———

Quicksilver.—The nimble sixpence.

———

To do business a man must have dollars and sense.

———

THE NEW Orleans *Picayune* expresses its belief that " if a bank officer would look at a burglar with a bag of tools as severely as he does at an honest man with a small note, many robberies might be prevented."

———

LOCAL.—A clever old lady who mourns the untimely end of our First National, thinks the *teller* of that bank was most awfully to blame. He ought to have *told* the people in time to save their money. She has now dis-covered that a teller isn't necessarily one who *tells*—all he knows.

———

California bankers tell us, the moon-eyed Celestial, when called on to pay, answereth, " I no havee, how can ?"

First City Man (contemplating sea-gull) : " There's happy creatures, Thomson. They've no acceptances to meet." *Second City Man :* " Ah ! my boy, it's all very well to talk so ; but, remember, Providence has ordained that they also have their bills to provide for."

———

Two hundred clerks of the Bank of France have petitioned the President of that institution for permission to wear their beards, a privilege now denied them.

———

Men who have made their fortunes are not those who have five thousand dollars given them to start with.

———

Money.—The missing link between man and his tailor.

———

The end of all commerce is individual gain.

———

" Situation wanted in a bank. Salary not so much an object as the combination of the safe."

———

It is said that Montana, with a population of 50,000, has not a business failure in a year. This circumstance is said to be due to the custom of hanging those who are unable to make satisfactory arrangements with creditors.

———

The number of moral failures without assets is alarmingly on the increase. As in the case of commercial failures, the nominal assets are quite imposing, but examination commonly results in finding an empty treasury.

————

An absent-minded and prominent New London grocer, who had been talking about potatoes, recently signed a check "—— Potatoes," and it went through several banks before the mistake was noticed.

————

" Riches take wings "—to Canada, generally.

————

If a bank cannot stand a loan it must eventually come down.

————

Bankers, like all creditors, "are a superstitious sect, —great observers of set days and times.".

————

. Quoth Solomon : " He that is surety for a stranger shall smart for it, and he that hateth suretyship is sure." Almost all who sign as surety have occasion to remember this, but they are nevertheless held liable upon their contracts, otherwise there would be no smarting, and the proverb would fail.

————

Mr. Murray says that " Heaven is not populated with singing thieves or palm-bearing bankrupts, who settle with their creditors at twenty-five cents on the dollar Wednesday, and ride to church the next Sabbath in a thousand-dollar coach, with a man in livery on the box." We believe this proposition to be incontestible.

Oh, what are the prizes we perish to win,
To the first little "shiner" we caught with a pin !
No soil upon earth is so dear to our eyes
As the soil we first stirred in terrestrial pies.

Next time a customer complains of the bad pens at the public desk, look wise, Mr. Cashier, and remark, "This is not a Pen-ny Bank."

Experience teaches us that insolvency is the normal state of mankind, and the payment of debts a disease which now and then breaks out.

A former Iowa banker, B. F. Allen, now lives at Leadville, in a log cabin 15x20 feet in size, containing three beds, a cook-stove, and limited furniture. But he has just paid $60,000 for a silver mine.

Says *Truth :* "One of the West End tailors was deploring, with a friend, the depression of trade. 'Depend upon it,' he said, 'when eminent bankers in Lombard street come to me to have their trousers reseated, there must be something very wrong with the money market.'"

"Can you write a good financial article?" said an editor-in-chief to a new man. "Oh, yes; that is my strong hold on the press," said the new man, and immediately sat down and dashed off a written promise to pay for a small amount of money. This he signed and handed in for inspection. The editor, after hurriedly glancing over the document, remarked that as he was running a conservative paper, he was not prepared to indorse all that the stranger had written, but that if he would go and prepare an obituary notice of himself, he would publish it with great pleasure. He has not been heard of since.

In Illinois, if any man steals any amount less than $15, he is sent to jail, and for stealing over $15 he is sent to the penitentiary ; but if he steals exactly $15, there is no penalty attached to the offense. The thieves out there are very careful to steal the exact amount to exempt them from punishment.

A Youngstown German got angry with a banker of that place for demanding a heavy discount, and when the banker asserted that it was "business," replied : " Pisiness? pisiness? You sit here all day and robs a man bare faced before his pack, and calls dat pisiness, ha ?"

Out in Kansas, when a bank closes its doors, they dispense with all such little formalities as receivers and expert accountants. A depositor puts a pistol to the president's head, another shoots the cashier, and half an hour later the institution is in good working order again.

It is curious that money should be called by so many

different names. Some describe it as "spondulix," some as "the stuff," some as "the sugar," some as "rhino," some as "spoons," some as "the ready," others as "brads." The French call it "*l'argent,*" the English "the needful," in Mexico "casting," in the South "rocks," in the East "tin," in the West "rags," in Canada it goes by the name of "spelter," hereabouts it is "short."

———

Stock-broker at city restaurant, reading his bill of fare : "What is this—Beef à la financière ?" Friend : "I suppose it is cut from a Stock Exchange Bull !"

———

An amusing instance of carrying religion into business, occurred some time since in this wise. A farmer went to a broker to buy some "governments." "What *denomination* will you have ?" asked the broker. The question was a poser, but the farmer was equal to the emergency, and replied, after a moment's reflection : "I guess I'll take part of 'em in Old School Presbyterian, just to please the old lady, but give me the heft of 'em in Freewill Baptist."

———

A prominent lawyer in town, who thinks that in time of alarm confidence should be shown in the banks, made a deposit of his entire property, as soon as he heard of the robbery yesterday. It amounted to $3.25, and included a counterfeit fifty-cent piece, a silver quarter with a hole in it, four Roman coins of the time of Tiberius, and a horse-car ticket. It is patriotic promptness like this that makes one proud even of a lawyer.

———

A Missouri gentleman who drew all his money out of the bank during the late panic, died suddenly the other day. His weeping relatives offer a large reward to any one who will find where he hid the money.

———

CURRENCY CONUNDRUM.—Why is national bank currency like an umbrella?   *—Ex.*

Responses thus :

A careless man—because it is easy to lose it.

A miser—because one dislikes to have to use it.

Nice young man—because one can make a spread with it.

A Wall street man—because it is the hardest to borrow when you want it most.

A poor man—because it don't take long to count all you've got.

An unlucky man—because you can't get it back when lent.

A jolly man—because it is very convenient when the big *dues* come.

To all which we add—because it is *the* thing to lay by for a rainy day.

———

A well-known girl of the period—Em Bezzle. Her near and dear relative—D. Fault. Her uncle—Ab Squatulate. Her father—Ske Dad-dle.

Comfortable quarters—silver twenty-five-cent pieces.

———

The three coins that exactly make a dollar.—One-half and two quarters.

———

"Be cautious and bold."
"Never have anything to do with an unlucky man or place."—ROTHSCHILD'S MOTTOES.

———

The first ladies employed in the National Treasury were appointed in 1862. There are now 1,300 in the departments of Washington, receiving salaries varying from $900 to $1,800 yearly.

———

"Did you ever dabble in stocks?" inquired a lawyer of a witness who was known to have fled from his native land to this asylum of the free. "Well, yes, I got my foot in 'em once in the old country," was the reply.

———

There is one financial scheme, on which all parties can unite, namely, the abolition of twenty-cent pieces.

———

The chief end of a savings-bank account—div-id–end.

———

A bank is *such* a dol-orous place.

———

Frogs were the original greenbacks, and since they first drew breath they have been inflationists.

A Salamanca man lost a package containing $500 a year ago, and found it last week when he emptied a straw-bed tick.

A young lady of Austin, Nevada, is waiting until silver goes to par, so that he will get her a new dress.

As an evidence of hard times it may be mentioned that a young man in this State wrote to every bank in Detroit offering to " be your kasheer for $20 per month and board ; " and no bank could give him a place.

He who is intimate on short acquaintance is apt to be short on intimate acquaintance.

Pope Innocent XI. was the son of a banker.

If you see a man skipping across the country rapidly and trying to avoid notice, arrest him. Ten to one it is some savings bank president.

XL-lent—$40 borrowed.

A country banker, rigorously accurate, thus quoted two lines of a hymn sung at a funeral :

" Ten thousand thousand (10,000,000) are their tongues,
But all their joys are one (1)."

––––––

A merchant who always tells the truth, and a genius who never lies, are synonymous to a saint.—LAVATER.

––––––

Why are cents separated from dollars by a point? To make sense, of course.

––––––

It is a remarkable peculiarity with debts that their *expanding* power continues to increase as you *contract* them.

––––––

Creditors are a superstitious set—great observers of set days and times.—FRANKLIN.

––––––

Little that is truly noble can be expected from one who is *ever* poring over his cash-book, or balancing his accounts.

––––––

Money in thy purse will ever be in fashion.—RALEIGH.

––––––

GOOD LIFE, LONG LIFE.

He liveth long who liveth well,
  All else is life but flung away ;
He liveth longest who can tell
  Of true things truly done each day.

Then fill each hour with what will last,
  Buy up the moments as they go ;
The life above, when this is past,
  Is the ripe fruit of life below.

Sow love, and taste its fruitage pure,
  Sow peace, and reap its harvest bright,
Sow sunbeams on the rock and moor
  And find a harvest-home of light.

H. BONAR.

GEO. E. BOWDEN, *President.*   GEO. S. OLDFIELD, *Vice President.*
H. C. PERCY, *Cashier.*

THE HOME SAVINGS BANK

OF

NORFOLK, VA.

Chartered under State Banking Laws, September, 1874.

DIRECTORS:

H. B. NICHOLS,	SAML. HOFFLIN,	GEO. E. BOWDEN.
F. RICHARDSON,	J. R. GILLETT.	S. E. BICKFORD.
B. F. BOLSOM,	CAPT. E. PICKUP,	GEO. S. OLDFIELD.
	REV. E. G. CORPREW.	

INTEREST ALLOWED ON SAVINGS DEPOSITS.

Interest-Bearing Certificates of Deposit issued, payable, if desired, in NEW YORK or BOSTON.

COLLECTIONS MADE ON ALL ACCESSIBLE POINTS IN VIRGINIA AND NORTH CAROLINA, AND REMITTED FOR AT LOWEST RATES ON DAY OF PAYMENT.

BILLS OF EXCHANGE DRAWN

On England, Ireland, France, Germany and Switzerland.

ON CITY COLLECTIONS we charge only current rate of exchange (except in cases of past due paper, involving extra trouble), and remit on day of payment, or advise of non-payment, with reasons, if any are given.

CORRESPONDENTS:

New York—NATIONAL SHOE AND LEATHER BANK.
Boston—BLACKSTONE NATIONAL BANK.
Philadelphia—SEVENTH NATIONAL BANK.
Baltimore—NATIONAL BANK OF BALTIMORE.
Washington—NATIONAL BANK OF THE REPUBLIC.
Chicago—PRESTON, KEAN & CO.
Richmond—STATE BANK OF VIRGINIA.

BANKER'S PUBLICATIONS.

13
SPRUCE
ST.

BRADFORD RHODES & CO., PUBLISHERS, NEW YORK.

[LIST AND PRICES OVER.

BRADFORD RHODES & CO.,

PUBLISHERS,

13 Spruce Street, New York.

RHODES' JOURNAL OF BANKING, a Monthly Magazine, of practical value to banks, bankers, dealers, investors, as well as the public interested in the monetary affairs of the country.

Terms: Five Dollars per annum, postage prepaid. Subscriptions terminate with current year. Fifty Cents a month for any unexpired part of a year.

Advertisements: Bank advertising only solicited. A quarter page $30 a year. Reduced rates for more space.

THE BANKER'S YEAR BOOK contains

1 — A new and correct list of the National Banks, State Banks, Private Bankers and Savings Banks of the United States, with their location, capital and surplus; the names of two or three officers, including assistant cashiers, (of National, State, or private banks), and the President, Secretary or Treasurer (of Savings Banks), and the names of other correspondents, in addition to the New York correspondent.

II.—A brief description of each city or town, where banks are located, having special reference to its trade facilities and commercial importance.

III.—A concise summary of laws in force in each State, relative to banking, collections, interest and general commercial dealings.

Terms $3 a Copy.

Advertisements and Special Notices of banks and bankers and such others as are directly to their interest, are inserted at the following rates: Card, 1½ inch space, $15; Quarter Page $25; Half Page $40; One Page $75.

Illustrations of bank buildings to appear in advertisements are engraved at our expense. We guarantee first-class illustrations. Proofs submitted for approval. Can be engraved from a photograph, print, drawing, or outline sketch.

The List of Banks and Bankers appearing in the "Banker's Year Book" receives the most careful attention. The work upon its revision proceeds all the time. Bank officers, bankers, and others interested in maintaining a list absolutely correct, are besought to lend their aid by promptly sending information regarding new institutions or changes, as well as by calling attention to any shortcomings.

The Safeguard and Savings Bank Reporter. $1 a year.
Banking Laws and Miscellaneous Books for Bankers.
Keyes' History of Savings Banks in the U. S. Octavo, 2 Vols., 480 and 636 pp. respectively. $5 per Vol. "The only reliable account of these institutions published."
Interest Tables, &c.

The above publications will be sent post-paid anywhere in the United States or Canada on receipt of price.

[OVER.]

THE BANKER'S MAGAZINE

AND

STATISTICAL REGISTER.

A monthly periodical of 80 to 96 pages, containing carefully prepared articles upon current financial topics, the principles of Finance and the Practice of Banking. The changing phases of affairs, domestic and foreign, touching monetary interests, are recorded and commented on, as they present themselves. Of the practical questions as to the duties and responsibilities of active banking, which continually arise, some are presented each month in the Inquiries of Correspondents, and are discussed in this Magazine. A department is specially devoted to the *Law* in its relation to Banks and Bankers, and all important decisions are reported, the opinion of higher courts being given in full whenever justified by the importance of the points involved. The constantly recurring changes among National and State Banks and private Bankers are promptly announced, the MAGAZINE thus furnishing, in connection with THE BANKER'S ALMANAC AND REGISTER, a freshly corrected record of the banks and bankers of the United States and Canada. The financial legislation of Congress is carefully noted, as also are the financial circulars and rulings of the Secretary of the Treasury and the Comptroller of the Currency.

A FULL INDEX furnishes a ready reference to the yearly volume, which begins with the number for July.

MONTHLY, FIVE DOLLARS PER ANNUM.

Single Numbers, Fifty Cents. Specimen Copies, Twenty-five Cents. For TEN DOLLARS will be sent, free of postage,

The Banker's Magazine for one year, . . .	Price $5 00		
The Banker's Almanac and Register for 1879, one copy	" 3 00		
National Bank Laws of the United States (New Edition)	" 1 00	$11.25	
Economies for Beginners, by Macleod (just issued)	" 1 00		
The Silver Question, by Geo. M. Weston .	" 1 25		

OR

The Banker's Magazine for the year 1879, The Banker's Almanac and Register, and The Banker's Common-place Book (Price $1.50), with either of the three books last named, for $10.

P. O. Box 4574. *I. S. HOMANS, Publisher, N. Y.*

THE
BANKERS' DIRECTORY

OF THE

UNITED STATES AND CANADA.

Issued Semi-annually, in January and July.

CONTAINS

**A COMPLETE AND CORRECTED LIST OF BANKS, BANKERS AND
SAVINGS BANKS IN THE UNITED STATES AND CANADA,
THEIR OFFICERS, CAPITAL, SURPLUS, NEW YORK
AND WESTERN CORRESPONDENTS.**

The Commercial Laws of each State and Territory, including the
Laws relating to Insolvency, Interest, Taxes, Notes
and Bills of Exchange, &c., &c.

A List of reliable Commercial Lawyers in the United States and
Canada, recommended by the different Banks,
&c., &c., &c., &c., &c., &c.

PRICE, THREE DOLLARS.

RAND, McNALLY & CO., PUBLISHERS,
77 and 79 Madison Street, Chicago, Ill.

1879.   1879.

G. W. CARLETON & CO.

NEW BOOKS

AND NEW EDITIONS,

RECENTLY ISSUED BY

G. W. CARLETON & Co., Publishers,

Madison Square, New York.

The Publishers, on receipt of price, will send any book on this Catalogue by mail, *postage free*

All books [unless otherwise specified] are handsomely bound in cloth, with gilt backs suitable for libraries.

Mary J. Holmes' Works.

Tempest and Sunshine....	$1 50	Darkness and Daylight.........	$1 50
English Orphans................	1 50	Hugh Worthington..............	1 50
Homestead on the Hillside.....	1 50	Cameron Pride.	1 50
'Lena Rivers	1 50	Rose Mather..	1 50
Meadow Brook	1 50	Ethelyn's Mistake...............	1 50
Dora Deane.....................	1 50	Millbank	1 50
Cousin Maude	1 50	Edna Browning..................	1 50
Marian Grey....................	1 50	West Lawn......................	1 50
Edith Lyle.....................	1 50	Mildred	1 50
Daisy Thornton.....(New)......	1 50	Forrest House....(New)........	1 50

Marion Harland's Works

Alone	$1 50	Sunnybank	$1 50
Hidden Path	1 50	Husbands and Homes....	1 50
Moss Side....	1 50	Ruby's Husband	1 50
Nemesis.........................	1 50	Phemie's Temptation..........	1 50
Miriam........................	1 50	The Empty Heart...........	1 50
At Last	1 50	Jessamine.	1 50
Helen Gardner.................	1 50	From My Youth Up..............	1 50
True as Steel....(New)...... ...	1 50	My Little Love.................	1 50

Charles Dickens—15 Vols.—"Carleton's Edition."

Pickwick, and Catalogue........	$1 50	David Copperfield................	$1 50
Dombey and Son................	1 50	Nicholas Nickleby.............	1 50
Bleak House....	1 50	Little Dorrit	1 50
Martin Chuzzlewit............	1 50	Our Mutual Friend............	1 50
Barnaby Rudge—Edwin Drood.	1 50	Curiosity Shop—Miscellaneous..	1 50
Child's England—Miscellaneous.	1 50	Sketches by Boz—Hard Times..	1 50
Christmas Books—Two Cities...	1 50	Great Expectations—Italy.......	1 50
Oliver Twist—Uncommercial...	1 50		
Sets of Dickens' Complete Works, in 15 vols.—[elegant half calf bindings]..		50 00	

Augusta J. Evans' Novels.

Beulah.........................	$1 75	St. Elmo........	$2 00
Macaria	1 75	Vashti..............	2 00
Inez............................	1 75	Infelice ....(New)............	2 ..

May Agnes Fleming's Novels.

Guy Earlscourt's Wife	$1 50	A Wonderful Woman	$1 50
A Terrible Secret	1 50	A Mad Marriage	1 50
Norine's Revenge	1 50	One Night's Mystery	1 50
Silent and True	1 50	Kate Danton	1 50
Heir of Charlton—(New)	1 50	Carried by Storm....(New)	1 50

The Game of Whist.

Pole on Whist—The English standard work. With the "Portland Rules.".....$1 00

Miriam Coles Harris.

Rutledge	$1 50	The Sutherlands	$1 50
Frank Warrington	1 50	St. Philips	1 50
Louie's Last Term, St. Mary's	1 50	Round Hearts for Children	1 50
Richard Vandermarck	1 50	A Perfect Adonis—(New)	1 50

Mrs. Hill's Cook Book.

Mrs. A. P. Hill's New Southern Cookery Book, and domestic receipts....$2 00

Julie P. Smith's Novels.

Widow Goldsmith's Daughter	$1 50	The Widower	$1 50
Chris and Otho	1 50	The Married Belle	1 50
Ten Old Maids	1 50	Courting and Farming	1 50
His Young Wife	1 50	Kiss and be Friends—(New)	1 50

Victor Hugo.

Les Miserables—From the French. The only complete unabridged edition.....$1 50

Captain Mayne Reid.

The Scalp Hunters	$1 50	The White Chief	$1 50
The Rifle Rangers	1 50	The Tiger Hunter	1 50
The War Trail	1 50	The Hunter's Feast	1 50
The Wood Rangers	1 50	Wild Life	1 50
The Wild Huntress	1 50	Osceola, the Seminole	1 50

Artemus Ward.

Complete Comic Writings—with Biography, Portrait. and 50 Illustrations....$1 50

A. S. Roe's Select Stories.

True to the Last	$1 50	A Long Look Ahead	$1 50
The Star and the Cloud	1 50	I've Been Thinking	1 50
How Could He Help it?	1 50	To Love and to be Loved	1 50

Charles Dickens.

Child's History of England—Carleton's New "*School Edition*," Illustrated..$1 25

Hand-Books of Society.

The Habits of Good Society—The nice points of taste and good manners. ..$1 00
The Art of Conversation—for those who wish to be agreeable talkers..........1 00
The Arts of Writing, Reading, and Speaking—For self-improvement... ..1 00
New Diamond Edition—Elegantly bound. 3 volumes in a box.................3 00

Carleton's Popular Quotations.

Carleton's New Hand-Book—Familiar Quotations, with their authorship.....$1 50

Famous Books—"Carleton's Edition."

Arabian Nights—Illustrations	$1 00	Don Quixote—Dore Illustrations	$1 00
Robinson Crusoe—Griset. do..	1 00	Swiss Family Robinson. do...	1 00

Josh Billings.

His Complete Writings—With Biography, Steel Portrait, and 100 Illustrations.$2 00
Old Probability—Ten Comic Almanax, 1870 to 1879. Bound in one volume. ...1 50

Allan Pinkerton.

Model Town and Detectives	$1 50	Spiritualists and Detectives	$1 50
Strikers, Communists, etc	1 50	Mollie Maguires and Detectives	1 50
Criminal Reminiscences, etc	1 50	The Mississippi Outlaws, etc..	1 50

Celia E. Gardner's Novels.

Stolen Waters. (In verse)	$1 50	Tested	$1 50
Broken Dreams. (Do.)	1 50	Rich Medway's Two Loves	1 50
Terrace Roses	1 50	A Woman's Wiles	1 50
A New Novel	1 50		

Carleton's Popular Readings.

Selected Prose and Poetry—Edited by Mrs. Anna Randall-Diehl...... ...... $1 50

www.ingramcontent.com/pod-product-compliance
Lightning Source LLC
Chambersburg PA
CBHW021120270326
41929CB00009B/967